The Executive's Role in
Knowledge Management

Carla O'Dell
with Paige Leavitt

APQC
PUBLICATIONS

APQC
123 North Post Oak Lane, Third Floor
Houston, Texas 77024

Edited by Emma Skogstad
Designed by Connie Choate and Fred Bobovnyk Jr

Manufactured in the United States of America

ISBN 1-932546-13-8

APQC
Web site address: www.apqc.org

TABLE OF CONTENTS

P R E F A C E

The world is getting smaller. Time is getting shorter. Networks are getting larger and more complex. And your stakeholders are demanding more. Do you thrive in this environment? This book is for senior managers who are molding their companies and agencies into learning organizations. For those who grasp the potential of their organizations' knowledge assets and want to develop strategies for leveraging them, this book can act as a guidebook. For those who are actively involved in crafting their organization's knowledge-based business strategy, this book offers the perspectives of leaders who have faced this challenge and succeeded. For those who want to use knowledge and learning to support existing core competencies, as well as create new ones, this book offers leading examples. Most importantly, this book is for senior managers who lead by example and want to adapt successful approaches that will result in significant gains.

By discussing the role of executives in 1) establishing the need for a knowledge management (KM) initiative, 2) ensuring a solid business case, 3) steering for tangible measures, 4) creating a framework for technology support, 5) cultivating a knowledge-sharing culture, and 6) becoming the face of an internal communications strategy, this book outlines the most critical success factor in knowledge management success: senior-level support.

With proven practices, advice from executives, and straight-forward guiding principles, this book can help senior managers throughout their journey to become a learning organization. This book is also useful for KM practitioners who must establish a credible business case to gain senior-level support.

The advice in this book is based on almost a decade of research conducted by Dr. Carla O'Dell and the American Productivity & Quality Center (APQC). An internationally recognized resource for process and performance improvement, APQC helps organizations adapt to rapidly changing environments, build new and better ways to work, and succeed in a competitive marketplace. APQC works with organizations to identify best practices; discover effective methods of improvement; broadly disseminate findings; and connect individuals with one another and with the knowledge, training, and tools they need to succeed. Founded in 1977, APQC serves organizations around the world in all sectors of business, education, and government. APQC has conducted research and KM projects with more than 300 organizations since 1995. Most of what you see being practiced as knowledge management around the world has been dramatically influenced by participation in those consortia and the reports APQC has published. It is a bold claim, but one that APQC feels is justified.

In 1995 APQC conducted the nation's largest symposium on KM. Based on issues raised at the symposium, APQC launched—under O'Dell's direction—its first consortium study, *Emerging Best Practices in Knowledge Management*. Most recently, O'Dell served as the subject matter expert for studies on measuring the impact of KM and the transfer of best practices.

O'Dell currently heads APQC's efforts to help clients design and implement knowledge management and best practices transfer initiatives. Consequently, she and APQC have shared knowledge with thousands of KM practitioners, while helping organizations use best practices to design and implement knowledge management strategies that get results. (For information on APQC's resources in knowledge management, please see page 127.)

Like its membership base, APQC's work in knowledge management stretches across industries and around the globe. APQC's members are from various sectors and of various sizes, and most of them operate globally. APQC has researched knowledge management best practices in the defense, automotive, banking, energy, technology, consulting, education, health, manufacturing, pharmaceutical, retail, and telecommunications industries, as well as the government sector, to name just a few.

This book draws on APQC's years of research and pares down the information to the guiding principles and proven practices that will help senior managers set sensible, yet aggressive, expectations and goals for a knowledge management initiative.

INTRODUCTION

No business can ignore the need to manage what it knows. During the 1990s, a number of business principles gained attention as efforts "critical to your organization's success." However, unlike other opportunities for a competitive advantage, knowledge management became a mode of operations for leading organizations. Now, more than 80 percent of major corporations have explicit knowledge management initiatives, and global organizations now have hundreds of communities of practice. The *Journal of International Marketing* estimated that spending on knowledge management was approximately $12 billion USD in 2003.

Through capturing lessons learned, reusing designs, transferring best practices, and enabling collaboration and access to expertise, knowledge management has become a widely adopted business practice and imperative. Knowledge management is a systematic process of connecting people to people and people to the knowledge and information they need to act effectively and create new knowledge.

I commonly see on executives' agendas the desire to increase responsiveness to customers, identify cost redundancies, improve new product/service development, improve the quality and productivity of work, and make better decisions. A response to these challenges will require use of an organization's best knowledge assets by a whole organization. That systematic capture, transfer, and use of internal and external know-how is a vital part of any business strategy.

- With no common processes for sharing information among employees, partners, and customers, limited information exchange will occur among suppliers and the engineering, manufacturing, and service functions. Consequently, the organization will experience ineffective design reuse, and product launch mistakes will be repeated.
- If there is no company standard expertise locator or people finder, then the inability to locate subject matter experts will result in lost opportunities, lost time, and being incapable of applying the right resources to significant problems. And with too many different systems, proposals, and pricing sheets, sales representatives cannot

We need to focus information, channel it, convert it to knowledge, understand this knowledge, and then, based on that understanding, make sound business decisions. That is why knowledge management is very important: to be able to capture more value.

— Saad Bargach, then-president of drilling and measurements, Schlumberger Oilfield Services, speaking at APQC's conference *Next-generation Knowledge Management.*

From every conceivable corner of the Halliburton world. From people at every career level, in every conceivable department. I never expected this kind of response. And I must admit that I didn't think there were more than a few "new" ideas out there in the world. Proof once again that I do not have all the answers, but together we all do.

— Dave Lesar, CEO, Halliburton Energy Services Group, commenting during the APQC study *Measuring the Impact of Knowledge Management* on the overwhelming response to his request for new ideas from Halliburton employees.

Our business challenge was that we had growth expectations that say we are going to do two or three times the level of output in new products with less than a 40 percent increase in resources. We already knew that people were working about as hard as they possibly could work, so the answer "just work harder" was not going to work really well. We needed to do things differently.

— Todd K. Abraham, vice president of strategic technology and knowledge management, the Pillsbury Company, speaking at APQC's conference *Knowledge Management: Lessons from the Leading Edge.*

Of all the initiatives we've undertaken at Chevron during the 1990s, few have been as important or as rewarding as our efforts to build a learning organization by sharing and managing knowledge throughout our company. In fact, I believe this priority was one of the keys to reducing our operating costs by more than $2 billion per year—from about $9.4 billion to $7.4 billion—over the last seven years.

— Ken Derr, retired chairman, Chevron Corp., a member of APQC's Board of Directors.

have access to information they need when they need it. This can prolong the sales cycle and lead to less-than-best sales solutions offered to the client.

- With retirement and turnover, knowledge is walking out the door everyday. New hires do not have the benefit of past experiences and lessons learned, yet their time-to-competence needs to be compressed.
- Mergers and acquisitions result in two bodies of knowledge and expertise and two cultures that must assimilate quickly.
- Portals and e-business are drivers of knowledge management. People want information they can use and trust from a single point of access. Also, an often neglected point is that customers want access to your knowledge and to their business transactions with you.
- Another driving factor is e-learning. Firms now must know where and how knowledge is really being created and acquired. Knowledge management can set the framework for how learning fits into the overall picture of developing employees and making them productive.

Despite these pressing needs, knowledge is sticky. Without a systematic process and enablers, it will not move.

A knowledge management initiative enhances the performance of the organization and its people. The goal is not to share knowledge for its own sake, although that is a valuable byproduct of the process. The goal is to enhance organizational performance by explicitly designing and implementing tools, processes, systems, structures, and cultures to improve the identification, capture, validation, and transfer knowledge critical for decision making.

Since APQC began focusing on knowledge management in 1995, the KM arena has evolved rapidly in both scope and practice. The most significant change has been in the business community's level of understanding. Eight years ago, we did not have tools to analyze how knowledge flows in an organization; we did not have the methodologies for improving the flow and use; and we did not even know how to see the work of the organization in terms of what was productive knowledge to manage. Today, KM has come of age.

The formulation of crisp methodologies and the ability to blend various approaches to KM to tackle real business problems has made a dramatic difference.

The second major development is a growing recognition of the need to apply knowledge management thinking to virtually every other business issue and process. This trend is evident, for example, in APQC's recent benchmarking report investigating how knowledge management can be applied to Six Sigma and Lean, both major improvement initiatives (APQC, *Replicating the Gains of Six Sigma and Lean*, 2004). Six Sigma is not part of KM, but KM principles should help organizations get maximum leverage from the Six Sigma projects by transferring the lessons to more locations. This approach represents a new level of maturity for KM, and the value proposition is in the hundreds of millions of dollars for a large organization.

The third major development is the creation of user-friendly technologies for collaborating and for accessing information. The tools are powerful, but the methods and processes for collaborating across time and space and functions are just now beginning to emerge. Best practice is certainly not yet widespread.

Finally, the myth that you cannot measure KM has been dispelled. Knowledge itself is intangible and difficult to measure, but the impact of actively managing knowledge is far easier to gauge. The key to identifying the effects of knowledge management is to start with a business's desired outcome and work back from there. By stringing together this chain, you have a measurement system with clear, direct correlations.

As the processes, tools, and adoption of knowledge management continue to expand, senior managers are rightly asking: "What investments are we making in knowledge management? Are they enough? Too much? What are we getting for our money? What outcomes are we achieving, and what could we expect if we invest more?"

I have found that with a systematic approach, these questions can be answered. The purpose of this book is to help you, as a senior manager, ask the right questions and know what the answers mean so you can make decisions about where and how to invest.

Why Senior Leader Support Is Critical

Senior managers are role models for the values and principles that support the development of a learning organization.

— APQC's benchmarking report
Knowledge Management and the Learning Organisation: A European Perspective

Executive sponsorship is necessary for the success of a major initiative. ... As one company representative put it "Senior management must play a role in removing barriers, making learning a priority, and eliminating the negative impacts of sharing." Another reason why senior management sponsorship matters is that for the linkage to strategy to succeed, the senior leadership of the organization must be tied to the initiative.

— APQC's benchmarking report
Using Information Technology to Support Knowledge Management

The behavior of leaders, particularly senior leaders, often has a strong impact on the others in the organization. Leaders influence others directly by the expectations they set for others in the organization. Moreover, they influence people indirectly as role models.

— APQC's benchmarking report
Creating a Knowledge-Sharing Culture

In every knowledge management benchmarking study APQC has organized, one key finding consistently surfaces: the support of senior leaders is the primary critical success factor. In APQC's very first consortium benchmarking study on knowledge management in 1996, simply called *Knowledge Management*, we reported that executive support, usually gained by compelling competitive needs, is essential. One organization we studied that did not receive support was not able to fully deploy its approach. In contrast, the CEOs of several of our benchmarking partners were zealots about the value of knowledge and sharing of best practices. It was obvious from the responses to the question "What are the major drivers that help create a knowledge-sharing culture?" that the best-practice organizations were reaping the most gains from the CEO's vision.

In the years that followed, we found hundreds of examples to support that finding. In the benchmarking report *Using Information Technology to Support Knowledge Management*, the World Bank reported: "Management sponsorship is essential. It is important to get senior management involved and educated. Senior management must play a role in removing barriers by making learning a priority and eliminating the negative impacts of sharing." The World Bank has one of the world's most comprehensive and sophisticated knowledge management efforts, so the weight of this statement comes to bear. NASA also noted in the benchmarking report *Using Knowledge Management to Drive Innovation* that it was extremely important for it to get executives' support and broad sponsorship to make it easier to achieve cultural change, to deploy systems and solutions, and to transition and infuse knowledge management into day-to-day processes and activities.

A knowledge management system requires sustained intervention from leaders throughout an organization. Executives are in a unique position to drive such change. They are also in the best position to objectively determine whether successful practices are transferring and whether the organization is getting value. Executive involvement lends credibility to knowledge management principles and ensures the effort will be long term. Leading by example, executives shape the values of the organization and establish a support system to initiate and manage change. Without direction from management, knowledge management support tools, such as a portal, are unlikely to be aligned with the business strategy or to be fully capitalized on for an intended purpose. Executives ensure that a knowledge management initiative exists to support the big picture.

With such weight put on the shoulders of executives, it is encouraging to see that executives throughout large organizations have taken a more preemptive approach to knowledge management and not waited for grassroots efforts to proceed without an organization-wide vision. Enthusiasm like this is but one characteristic of leaders in organizations with the most successful knowledge management initiatives.

A couple of years ago, I heard the president of Best Buy Co., Brad Anderson, make an interesting note at an APQC conference. He said a company's leadership has to actively exhibit two characteristics: "The first is that leadership has the humility to know it does not have the answers, and the second is that leaders have the desire to listen."

I think that desire to learn, on the part of executives, is important not only as an example to employees, but also as a sign that the leaders are dedicated to cultivating a knowledge-sharing culture. I've found that senior managers truly committed to learning most likely have already laid the groundwork for a knowledge-sharing culture. (These same leaders are also more likely to allocate adequate resources to support knowledge management.)

As our needs of executives evolve, they must respond quickly and embrace learning opportunities. In the article "Role of Leadership in the Management of Corporate Knowledge," J.A. Kok astutely observes that effective senior managers realize "that effective management is not a matter of having the most knowledge; but knowing how to use it. It is not enough to know modern management concepts, but how they get implemented is equally important."

As you can imagine, for a company that has over $15 billion in annual revenues and is now acquiring other companies and that runs in businesses ranging from music software to appliances, that's a very diverse pool of knowledge. And nobody can have anything close to all of it. It's geographically spread out over the United States and soon internationally, so how do we get it in a place where we have that knowledge just at the right period of time?
— Brad Anderson, president, Best Buy Co., speaking at APQC's conference *Taking Knowledge and Best Practices to the Bottom Line.*

An Executive Task

Managers' power base is their relative level of knowledge. ... Managers no longer manage people or even knowledge, but the space in which knowledge is created. This space is both the intangible culture and the tangible environment, such as the office. ... If the managers succeed in managing their invisible balance sheets, they are promised a new world of increasing returns.

— Karl-Erik Sveiby, principal of Sveiby Knowledge Associates, in *"A Vision for the Knowledge Organisation in the Knowledge Era"*

Knowledge management can produce outstanding gains. For instance, Ford's Best Practice Replication process is built around communities of practice, which include people in each plant or facility who help identify, share, and transfer practices. More than $1 billion USD in documented bottom-line savings have been achieved since 1995, with a large number of additional benefits and savings measured and reported by communities but not certified for financial impact. Ford has now integrated Best Practice Replication into its Six Sigma initiative to ensure gains from Six Sigma projects are leveraged across the corporation.

Ford is not alone in its success. For instance, IBM has saved $50 million USD a year just in travel costs avoidance through virtual collaboration. It has also saved $6 million USD annually by finding information more quickly through its KM initiative. Caterpillar examined two of its communities of practice and found they generated $1.5 million USD from using a single KM network tool. This was, respectively, an ROI of 212 percent and 738 percent. (I detail how they got these great results in Chapter 5.)

As such gains become more common, shareholders in organizations in all industries will turn to their executives for similar results. As the records for company leaders become tied to their performance in leveraging knowledge assets, they must ask themselves: "Can I afford not to get involved in implementing knowledge management efforts? What is the cost of not sharing knowledge?" With the professional fate of executives tied to their companies' success, every executive will benefit from ensuring that sound operating principles are applied to his or her KM initiative's design and implementation.

The bottom line is this: For good results, develop a vision for the knowledge management initiative. For exceptional results, translate that vision into explicit expectations and demand tangible results. Executive involvement begets success.

This book examines both the role of senior leaders and realistic expectations for those executing the knowledge management implementation plan. Chapter 1 explains the basics of knowledge management, including the stages of implementation, roles, and framework. This information is supplemented by a glossary of terms and additional resources at the end of the book. Chapter 2 details how to define the organizational needs and, because knowledge management should not be partitioned into tiny buckets, how to use knowledge management to support major business opportunities. I detail what to demand in the business case, what executives need to know to get the most impact from knowledge management, and how to align expectations with aggressive goals and present capabilities. Chapter 3 details the necessary support structure, in terms of technology, for implementation and how executives are involved. Chapter 4 is devoted to the important issues of culture and change management and the executive's considerably important role in cultivating a knowledge-sharing culture and the appropriate communications strategy to support that effort. Chapter 5 is a collection of case studies of significant successes.

Once you have all of this information in your hands, I'll end with a little push: advice on how you can move forward.

CHAPTER I

Knowledge Management in Action

This chapter begins with an introduction to the basic tenets of knowledge management and describes how to set them in motion through the stages of implementation. It also describes the many roles in implementation, beginning with the executive's.

Introduction to Knowledge Management Principles

Knowledge management requires managers to work with complex and evolving issues, but there are some enduring characteristics and principles of KM that are important to know.

1. It is important not to confuse the terms *data, information,* and *knowledge*. Data can be facts and figures presented out of context. Although data can trigger innovation or improve efficiency, it lacks inherent meaning and provides no sustainable basis for action. Information, on the other hand, is data presented in context so people might make use of it. Information sources may include: patents, trademarks, processes, manuals, drawings, reports, research, transaction data, and market research. Thomas Davenport defines knowledge as "information combined with experience, context, interpretation, and reflection." I would define knowledge as information in action that people can make use of, along with the rules and context of its use. Valuable knowledge is embedded in language, stories, concepts, rules, and tools. Sources of knowledge can include your customers, products, and processes; rules of thumb; skills and experiences; know-how; and pinpointing "how things work around here."

2. Knowledge comes in two basic varieties: explicit and tacit, which are also known as formal/codified and informal/uncodified knowledge. Only 20 percent of what an organization contains is explicit. Explicit knowledge is easier to document and share, contributes to efficiency, and easier to replicate. It comes in the form of books and documents, formulas, project reports,

contracts, process diagrams, lists of lessons learned, case studies, white papers, policy manuals, etc. Explicit knowledge may not be useful without the context provided by experience. That means that 80 percent of what an organization knows is tacit in that it is harder to articulate, steal, and transfer. Tacit/Uncodified knowledge can be found through interactions with employees and customers and through the memories of past vendors. Management of tacit knowledge calls for different processes from explicit knowledge management. This knowledge is hard to catalog, highly experiential, difficult to communicate and document in detail, ephemeral, and transitory. It is also the basis for judgment and informed action. Tacit knowledge leads to competency and a higher competitive advantage. Firms concerned about knowledge loss fear that tacit knowledge has not been captured (made explicit) or transferred so that others may benefit from it.

3. Established organizations are typically swimming in enormous amounts of tacit and explicit knowledge, only some of which is valuable and durable enough to offer future competitive advantage and justify the costs of retaining and transferring it. The challenge is to determine exactly what and where that knowledge is and how it can be captured and transferred. The approaches for explicit knowledge may be more mechanical; those for tacit knowledge are more difficult.

4. Knowledge management is successful when information and knowledge move through the stages in *Figure 1* and are actually used.

5. Knowledge management initiatives succeed when executives aim efforts at a clear set of value propositions, such as improving customer-related practices, reducing time-to-market, or achieving new levels of operational excellence. The choice depends on the "value levers" in a particular marketplace.

6. If you build it, they will not necessarily come. Technology applications do not, in themselves, create a need or demand to change behavior or share knowledge. Technology is indispensable to knowledge management in modern organizations, but the road to effective knowledge management is littered with abandoned knowledge management "solutions" that were really just applications. These vehicles quickly run out of gas, if they start at

Figure 1

all. It is critical to select and implement technology as part of a larger, systematic knowledge management change initiative.

7. It is a myth that people hoard knowledge. What people hoard is their time and energy; they reserve it for high payoff activities. Most people want to share what they know; they want to learn from others and not repeat the mistakes of the past. The barriers to this are often structural: there is not enough time, the process is cumbersome, they do not know the source or the recipients and are not sure they can trust the information, and they know instinctively that tacit knowledge is richer than explicit knowledge. To ensure knowledge management is successful, work on these barriers, rather than on the psychological make-up of your employees.

8. Whenever possible, embed knowledge sharing, capture, and reuse into the work itself and provide value to those who participate. Employees should experience greater professional development and an easier time getting their work done correctly. Rewards and recognition are important, but they will not take the place of creating knowledge-sharing systems that work and provide value.

9. The transfer of best practices is the most common—and most effective—strategy. Every organization APQC has studied in its 13 KM consortium benchmarking studies relied on the transfer of internal best practices as a predominant KM strategy. It was not

the only strategy, but it was the most popular and effective way companies chose to find out and share what they know.

10. Cultivating a knowledge-sharing culture is the result of a successful knowledge management strategy. Some organizations are fortunate enough to start with a culture conducive to sharing knowledge, based on a strong professional ethic, corporate pride, and well-honed skills in teaming. However, this is not a prerequisite. Those organizations that do not have these cultural attributes need two prerequisites for building the culture of sharing: leadership support and practice.

11. Successful KM efforts typically employ a "push-me/pull-you" approach. A combination of push and pull strategies tends to work best. Push approaches are characterized by a desire to capture knowledge in central repositories and then push it out to the organization. In contrast, pull approaches expect people to seek the knowledge they need when they need it. Neither alone seems to be enough.

Setting KM Principles in Motion

Most KM approaches to address these needs fall into one or more of the following three categories (*Figure 2*). The categories vary by how much they focus on explicit compared to tacit knowledge and how much human interaction or technology is involved.

1. **Self-service plus**—This approach, which is focused on the knowledge worker, causes the greatest increase in individual knowledge worker productivity. Think of intranets, portals, expertise locator systems, search tools, and comprehensive content management systems. The object of self-service is to link employees at their desktop or work site to the information they need to do their job more effectively. Its value proposition, is that people can quickly access instructions, other people, or information in order to reduce their cycle time, avoid relearning, and diminish hassles. Critical success factors for this basic level of KM include good hardware and software embedded in the work space, an owner for each project and piece of content, the richness of the information and the ability to find it, and assistance from a helpdesk.

Types of KM Activities

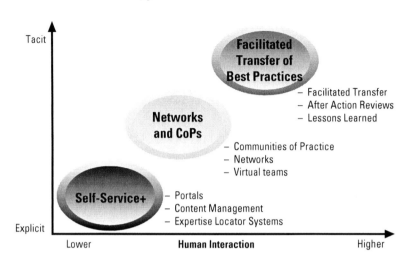

Figure 2

2. **Networks and communities of practice**—Access to information is important, but access to people with knowledge is more important. Groups of people, teams, communities of practice, and functions need to work together to create a shared space and shared objectives. This space could be physical (you do not have to use IT), or it could be virtual. The value proposition is to make simple tacit knowledge transfer possible. Communities of practice are probably the most ubiquitous KM approach. Critical success factors for communities include common purpose and need, as well as defined roles such as coordinators and moderators.

3. **Facilitated transfer of best practices**—This area has a huge return, but it also requires a significant investment. It refers to unit-to-unit and corporate-to-operating unit transfer of successfully demonstrated practices, which are things that we do, the way we handle orders, the way we handle hiring and firing, and the way we handle waste disposal. Opposed to the term *best practices*, some organizations prefer to standardize processes around the term *best-known method*. The value proposition is to close gaps and

raise everybody to the same level. Just because somebody tells you how to do something does not mean that you learned how to do it. You still have to put resources into changing your processes and your practices. The rule of thumb is not to use a heavy transfer process for a minor process that is not important to the organization. Instead, use communities to share tips and answers, and reserve the heavy duty transfer process for core business processes.

Obviously, implementation of a proper effort involves a lot of work. The reward for these efforts is significant results realized in targeted areas. Senior leaders can focus on achieving benefits, such as: increased employee and asset productivity, hastened organizational learning, better and faster decisions, an innovative workplace, and improved new product development and customer relations. Employees are more motivated by knowing they are operating with the best knowledge and experience held by the overall organization.

Now that you have these goals and basic principles in mind, as well as a very general understanding of the three categories of approaches to KM, I will cover the stages of implementation of a KM strategy and action plan.

Stages of Implementation

How do you successfully start a knowledge management initiative? You focus on a specific business need by targeting a value proposition. This may be achieving new product excellence by accelerating time-to-market, or it may be establishing customer loyalty by marketing, selling to, and serving customers more effectively. Some organizations use knowledge management for the wide-reaching goal of operational excellence through savings, process improvements, and new capacities. With this focus, organizations must frame their approach.

Based on our work with hundreds of organizations, APQC developed the Road Map to Knowledge Management Results: Stages of Implementation™ (**Figure 3**).

You can use this overview of the stages as a road map to understand where your organization is in the KM journey, to see how others have successfully faced similar challenges, and to learn what

APQC's Road Map to Knowledge Management Results: Stages of Implementation™

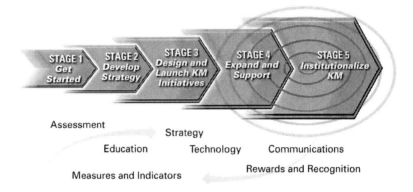

might be done to move forward. Understanding the issues, seeing the signposts of problems and opportunities, and knowing the tools and tactics of others can help at any stage. Learning from others provides the opportunity to "make new mistakes," not repeat those of others.

Each stage is described below as if it were distinct from the others. In reality, the stages flow into each other, as different parts of the organization move at different speeds and various elements fall into place. For example, not all organizations begin their journey with Stage 1. Sometimes Stage 2 happens because a manager simply wants to share knowledge in his of her business unit and sees knowledge management as the solution to a problem. Some organizations move through the stages very quickly by learning from early adopters and barely stopping to notice they have moved to a new level of implementation.

Stage 1: get started—Connect with a real business problem. Capitalize on the technology. Create a compelling picture and tell the stories.

In Stage 1, the fire to manage knowledge starts with the spark of inspiration. Someone—perhaps it is you—is inspired with the vision of what it would be like if your organization could effectively support knowledge capture, transfer, and use. This knowledge management champion, who is ideally a senior manager and often the manager of a single unit, begins to search for opportunities to share the vision with others and to find opportunities to demonstrate the value of KM to the organization.

The central tasks for the champion in Stage 1 follow.

1. **Make the concepts of knowledge management real** (through the way KM is defined and by providing data, storytelling, connecting to other initiatives, and benchmarking). The challenge is to create a tangible picture and clear understanding of what KM means to your colleagues and employees. The goal is to connect, at a personal level, with real issues, opportunities, and value surrounding the primary business strategy. Stay away from grand theoretical constructs.

2. **Identify others to join the cause.** The knowledge management champion and other advocates need to be great boundary-spanners so that the effort is not reduced to a single unit. Successful advocates find others by looking for groups that need to be connected and learning what the organization is already doing that is related to knowledge management.

3. **Look for windows of opportunity.** Seek out the biggest pain, gain, or opportunity to show the value and relevance of KM to your organization. This may involve enlisting the IT department to provide tools.

By the end of Stage 1, the champion, if successful, has created a compelling rationale or vision, engaged others in the cause, and has enough interested participants to form an exploratory group. If not already, an executive should ideally be on board by this point. This stage ends with a decision to explore KM in a more deliberate way.

Stage 2: develop strategy—Form a steering committee and cross-functional KM core group. Develop the knowledge management strategy. Select pilots and knowledge management initiatives. Dedicate resources.

Stage 2 is the turning point from individual interest or local efforts in KM to an organizational initiative, with guiding principles.

Best Buy's interest in KM originated as a desire to become a learning organization and avoid the mistakes of the past. In 1999 Brad Anderson, now chairman and CEO of Best Buy, challenged executives to find a way to make the concept of the learning organization real in a fast-moving retail environment. Best Buy created a steering committee of senior executives to authorize, guide, and fund the initiative and the KM initiative management office to coordinate all activities. The Best Buy steering committee adopted six guiding principles to direct the strategic approach and tactical decisions. KM efforts will:

1. support Best Buy's commitment to being a learning organization,

2. contribute to positive economic value for Best Buy,

3. support Best Buy in being customer-centric and the retailer of choice,

4. support Best Buy's goal of being the employer of choice,

5. involve knowledge-sharing tools that are ridiculously easy and enticing to use, and

6. make the lives of associates and customers easier.

It is characterized by the decision to explore "how KM might work here" and an evolution from individual passion to organizational action. The central task at this stage is to formulate the first iteration of the KM implementation strategy by determining how it fits with the business and conducting pilots to test the concept. This requires putting together a cross-function KM task force.

There is usually an obvious core group. The group is often made up of advocates enlisted in Stage 1 and other cross-functional representatives. The central tasks for the core group is to select pilots and find resources to support the pilots. These pilots will be used to test and learn how KM practices and principles can be applied in a selected focus area. The resources needed are primarily skilled staff members to facilitate the pilots and help employees discover a new way of working. (More on the KM core group follows later in this chapter.)

The Ford 2000 initiative, a key driver of knowledge-sharing efforts at Ford, was championed by the CEO and the president of the company. This initiative made Ford a more process-oriented company and requires information to be gathered along the production chain. Thus, each executive within the company is responsible for deploying a particular process. Because these processes are information intensive, people require knowledge sharing to do their work at Ford. According to Ford representatives, this is why knowledge-sharing efforts at the company do not require a formal champion. The Ford Best Practice Replication process operates with a small, core group of full-time staff and "focal points" in the business units.

Stage 3: design and launch—Form design teams. Launch the pilots and initiatives. Capture lessons learned.

Stage 3 signals the formal implementation of KM initiatives. Its goal is to provide evidence of KM's business value by conducting pilots and capturing lessons learn. These pilots will be most effective as the first step of a top-down approach, as opposed to grassroots efforts.

I am very much a supporter of top-down approaches to knowledge management, with significant employee involvement in design and implementation. These approaches bring faster results, better alignment with the overall business strategy, and technology consistency issues that business units would not originally contemplate. In the APQC benchmarking study *Retaining Valuable Knowledge*, we found that establishing executive support impacts the speed with which an organization can implement an effective knowledge management or retention initiative. The study revealed that partners whose initiatives started as grassroots took longer to develop their initiatives by at least two years. This extra time was most likely spent building the business case, developing champions for it, and securing resources (including funding). The bottom line is that most successful KM initiatives are the result of top-down approaches.

This top-down approach should include the flexibility for each business unit to adapt policy to how it works. Otherwise, no one will accept the mandate. And even in a top-down approach, it is wise to begin with focused, pilot efforts.

In Stage 3, pilots are important for leveraging lessons and addressing change management issues. Pick at least three pilots to start, with a mix of communities and projects, but do not pick more than you can support. At least one should be quick and visible, with potentially tangible and measurable results. It is critical to spotlight the functions that will yield the best results fastest.

In addition to having strategic alignment and measurable results, the pilot must also involve a group of people who are willing to reveal what they learned. If a group is afraid to share any failures with the KM core group and executives, then the pilot will not be a true learning opportunity for the planners. Finally, the majority of the lessons from the pilots should be transferable to other situations or business units.

Perhaps the most important task of this stage is to capture lessons learned: What made the early initiatives most successful? Are the results worth investing for expansion? Are people or units clamoring to be involved and to use the tools?

Stage 4: expand—Let the vision evolve. Develop an expansion strategy. Define governance and roles. Communicate and market the strategy. Create a balanced set of measures.

After the informative early initiative, Stage 4—the decision about the future of knowledge management—can go one of three ways:
1. expand and support the knowledge management efforts, in which case a strategy to proceed and budget are required;
2. improve the existing efforts, which usually leads to pushing the responsibility for maintenance of the initiatives back to the business units or to a function like IT; or
3. do nothing, which means the employees will often revert to prior behavior.

If KM has proved valuable enough to be officially expanded to become part of the organization's funded activities, then the resulting high visibility and authority will come—but as a mixed blessing.

The added visibility of costs and resources devoted to KM will require a more formal business evaluation and ROI justification. The good news is that unless unforeseen factors derail the efforts, KM is on its way to being considered a strategic and necessary competency. For this stage, remember to: create an expansion strategy and identify required resources, find where resources can be pulled (that is, who will benefit the most), vigorously communicate the strategy and rationale to the organization, and counter inevitable missteps through the KM core group.

Stage 5: institutionalize—With the entire organization recognizing knowledge management as "the way we work," senior leaders incorporate knowledge management into the business model. This involves realigning the structure, budget, and rewards and performance evaluation, while the KM core group continuously monitors and measures progress.

In some ways, Stage 5 is the continuation of Stage 4 to its logical conclusion of full enterprise-wide deployment. However, Stage 5 is unique in that it does not happen unless knowledge management is embedded in the business model, the organizational structure is realigned, and evidence of knowledge management competency becomes part of the formal performance evaluation.

Common Standards and Freedom to Innovate

My work, if I had to summarize it, is about giving agility, coherence, and capabilities to the organization.
— Hubert Saint-Onge, senior vice president of strategic capabilities, Clarica, speaking at APQC's conference *Showcasing Successful Knowledge Management Implementation*

Throughout all of the stages, the champions encourage the KM core group; pass on the passion; and look to avoid isolation of any units, potential reinvention, disconnected multiple initiatives, and regressing to where the organization started. One of the challenges of making knowledge management part of the business model is that divisions within the business certainly actualize the model in their own autonomous way. It is clear that knowledge management has to "go native" for acceptance, but it is also clear that some common standards and policies can help. Business need should drive the formulation of the policy, not the details of how a unit deploys it. The common institutional policy should allow variation where needed. The exception is for knowledge repositories that must be shared across the enterprise. As discussed in the introduction, the senior manager eager to see early success and quick expansion (for significant results) will take a more involved role in guiding the organization down the right path and pushing for results.

The Executive's Role in Implementation

It requires managers to move from a managing mindset to a leading mindset. In the end, the leaders work for the people. The objective is to provide the tools, the training, and the knowledge to the people to optimize flow. And the job of the manager is to say, Yes, I will go make that happen for you."
— Michael Joyce, then-vice president of best practices at Lockheed Martin Corp., presenting at APQC's conference *Showcasing Successful Knowledge Management Implementation*

In the initial stage, executives should focus KM on the value proposition and model being both behavior- and results-driven. This requires seeking out external information on current technology and successful support systems. Internally, it involves reviewing the company's existing technology infrastructure, searching for efforts that already align with knowledge management principles, and soliciting feedback. Essentially, senior managers must gauge what new behaviors will be required of employees and what support they will need.

With this information, executives can ensure that a knowledge management initiative exists to support the primary business strategies (more on this in Chapter 2). This may even involve selecting who will be on the KM core group to ensure success. With an eye on available resources, executives can expand or scale back the expectations of the

KM core group. Most importantly, by declaring explicit expectations and reviewing the business case for risks and tangibility (again, more on this in Chapter 2), executives set the critical solid foundation for knowledge-sharing efforts to become a valued mode of operations. As the initiative moves forward, executives provide ongoing support to the KM core group and are kept informed of progress. Throughout the design and implementation, executives will review measures reported by the KM core group that show the stages progressing efficiently and effectively. The group will depend on executives to eliminate barriers and encourage employees to change how they approach their work. As implementation progresses, a senior manager may also become the spokesperson for the effort, through formal and informal communications and rewards and recognition (more on this in Chapter 4).

From this short review of implementation, it is obvious that a KM core group will also play an integral role throughout the five stages of implementation. Let's review the group's role.

Why Do You Need a KM Core Group?

An executive cannot single-handedly make a firm a learning organization. He or she needs the support of respected champions in the business units. Here comes the first painful commitment in knowledge management. As with setting up any infrastructure, the effort will need people. This is where the senior managers take the leap from verbal direction to spending money on new roles and reallocating resources.

Knowledge management cannot be supported by a single librarian or tech support with a toll-free number. It involves support throughout the organizational structure, including analysts, network architects, knowledge managers, helpdesks, IT support, project teams, and community of practice leaders. But it begins with the KM core group.

In leading organizations, I have found that the role, reporting, budgets, and continuity staffing of the KM core group appear to be critical success factors for results. The KM core group is a group of knowledge management practitioners who centrally orchestrate the efforts. This group fulfills a need for involved project management and can alleviate confusions and missteps along the way.

Essentially, the role of the KM core group is to be knowledge management's process owner. This prevents redundant knowledge management efforts in the business units. Organizations create a KM core group, often a full-time staff, in order to integrate the knowledge management strategy into operations, to ensure that knowledge management activities do not occur in isolation, to give the knowledge management effort definition through a supporting framework and structure, and to identify the people and roles that will actually make it happen.

The KM core group is made of up employees from throughout the organization—including information technology, market research, sales, and human resources—with various expertise in communication, strategic and operational planning, culture, technology, customer value management, behaviors, and rewards. Not all need to be full-time assignments, but some should be. Executives greatly contribute to the initiative's success by involving themselves in the selection of the KM core group and ensuring the group is well rounded with committed personnel. Beyond the résumé, the right attitude will include an openness to learning and sharing, listening, networking, advocating, and taking risks.

The KM core group's responsibilities evolve as the initiative progresses through the stages of implementation. (See side bar below.) As the group carries out its responsibility to coordinate other staff, the knowledge management staffing model will begin to mirror the organization's structure. The KM core group will oversee and catalyze strategy and approaches. Business units staff the day-to-day work of the communities of practice and networks, as well as manage their own content online. Business units eventually provide knowledge champions and brokers who actually serve as the field consultants and leaders to the local or community initiatives. The KM core group coordinates these activities but does not staff them.

Business units should increasingly play an active role in staffing knowledge management activities; this is highly desirable from both a quality and commitment perspective. Each functional unit needs the flexibility to determine what works best for it. The business unit members know more about what these business needs and social dynamics are, who the experts are, and where resources can be found.

The evolving roles of the KM core group are to:
- flesh out the business case and adhere to strategic direction based on business needs;
- analyze costs and the infrastructure required;
- design roll-out plans and institutionalize common processes;
- plan projects and coordinate knowledge management activities and resources;
- recommend communication, training, rewards, and other issues affecting cultural acceptance of a knowledge management approach;
- coordinate the other staff needed, with specific roles, measures, recognition, and training;
- provide methodologies, including measurement support; and
- provide a central staff of internal consultants to launch new initiatives, partner with the business groups to launch them, and then monitor them over time.

In APQC's recent benchmarking study *Measuring the Impact of Knowledge Management*, we found that all of the best-practice partners studied rely on the business units for key staffing positions, either in full-time or part-time roles. Typically, business units pay directly for staff time; they provide the knowledge champions and brokers. But because these units have indicated a lack of willingness and/or time to measure results, the KM core groups actually go to the business units and find and report the measures themselves. This may seem like a lot of work for the KM core groups; however, study partners reported a limited amount of time spent on measurement efforts. Fifty percent of the study partners dedicated only six to ten hours per month to this activity.

What About a Steering Committee or Council of Executives?

Many organizations have found it helpful to establish a steering committee or council of executives to guide, fund, and validate the value proposition and the strategic intent of the knowledge management initiative. This is usually the same executive group that commissioned and approved the business case.

Steering committees provide support in a myriad of ways, such as guiding the KM core group in the development of the implementation plan and business case, funding, minimizing barriers, approving initiatives, communicating their views on knowledge management, and promoting knowledge sharing throughout the enterprise. The steering committee acts as the bridge between the knowledge management initiative and the formal organization. The steering committee links the business units, corporate functions, and IT together, which ensures that the organizational strategy dictates the scope and direction of the knowledge retention initiative, rather than the preferences of any one business unit or group.

The role of a steering committee is to create purpose and context, legitimize certain activities and forbid others, and set direction. During the planning and development phase, a steering committee guides the scope of the initiative through sponsorship, funding, and monitoring in order to align the initiative with the business strategy. As design and development begins, the steering committee drops into the background unless major issues arise.

The committee is also notified of the progress of the initiative. During deployment, the steering committee can be the evangelists by spreading the news of the initiative throughout the organization and modeling behavior that encourages participation.

Some leading roles often found on this committee follow.

- **CKO**—The role of the chief knowledge officer varies greatly in terms of knowledge management initiatives. Often, this figure is the senior-most manager, who is guiding the entire effort. In some organizations, often where the CEO has initiated the knowledge management effort, the CKO is actually tasked with heading the KM core group. Regardless of whether the CKO is wearing the senior manager hat or the group leader hat, this person is a key coordinator of knowledge management activities. Unlike most members of the KM core group with a specific functional interest, this role is focused on aligning behaviors and support structures with primary business strategies.

- **CIO**—The chief information officer, who focuses on physical computer and network assets, brings realistic expectations for what is hoped of an organization's existing infrastructure and what is possible to develop or buy. Strategic alignment is necessary for every element of a knowledge management initiative, including the technology. At the chief level, this person has the ability to ensure the full support of any technology-focused functional unit.

All of these roles cultivate a work environment that delivers value to the organization. Additionally, they create clear processes, classification schemes, and tools that promote knowledge sharing across boundaries.

The rest of this book refers to "executive" leadership, which can either be a single champion or the group that operates as a steering committee. With all of this information in hand, you are prepared to support the business strategy through a solid business case for knowledge management.

At Schlumberger, the steering committee consists of individuals: the Schlumberger communications manager, the oilfield services marketing manager, the manager of the content management system, the e-business manager, and the knowledge management manager. At Schlumberger, this steering committee is also part of the KM core group and owns the content management initiatives. This committee is intimately involved in all phases of the knowledge management initiative. Management sponsors of the content management initiatives were either the CEO or his direct reports

C H A P T E R   2

Supporting the Business Strategy

Bob Buckman, retired president of Buckman Laboratories, built his successful KM strategy around the simple premise that moving knowledge around is more efficient than moving people around. From this premise (and expectation of cost savings), he was able to build a focused expectation for knowledge management. This chapter discusses how to link knowledge management to business needs, what to demand in the knowledge management business case, and how to gauge the tangible results of your funding and allocation of resources. I also answer the critical question: What is this going to cost?

Focus Knowledge Management on the Business Strategy

The *Journal of Business Strategy* reported in 2002 that 85 percent of organizations with knowledge management initiatives conceded that their KM initiatives had no stated objectives. This shows a major misstep on the part of many senior managers to regard knowledge management as a separate effort, instead of as a tool to enable the most important elements of the business strategy. In fact, the most compelling reason for senior managers to become involved in their organizations' knowledge management effort in the first place is to ensure that knowledge-sharing activities relate to the overall business strategy. Managing knowledge has to be part of the business model and embraced as offering a competitive advantage or else it is highly unlikely to become an enterprise-wide mode of operations.

In addition, organizations that have not tied knowledge management efforts to business objectives lack tangible measures of results that are valued across the organization. Instead, these organizations are susceptible to being misled by technology vendors with wide-reaching products to sell. These products and their purposes are secondary to aligning knowledge management efforts with the business strategy.

American Management Systems Inc.: cultivating a knowledge-sharing culture—Executives reinforce a visible connection between knowledge sharing and the business strategy at American Management Systems, an international business and information technology consulting company that caters to corporations and government agencies. For example, there are several strategic initiatives that came directly out of American Management Systems' knowledge centers. One of these initiatives involves how American Management Systems can effectively manage large engagements with more than 100 people involved. To address this issue, American Management Systems held a workshop at the first knowledge centers conference to bring together the best thinkers who are managing large projects to figure out what is working. The chairman participated in this meeting, and as a result of this collaboration, he and other senior executives established a new framework for managing large engagements. This major strategic initiative resulted in a fundamental rethinking of engagement management at American Management Systems and even created a new functional role: the engagement manager.

Halliburton: improving service quality—One of the world's largest providers of oil field services, Halliburton has operations in more than 100 countries. In late 2001 Halliburton's knowledge management group was formed to take on the challenge of improving service quality and providing customers with the right solution at the right level of performance. Halliburton had found that 30 percent to 40 percent of the time, knowledge or information was not flowing to the people in the field who needed it to perform to the desired level of reliability and quality. Halliburton's knowledge management initiative was designed to avoid or quickly solve service quality problems and to share solutions more quickly among key communities selected for their impact on the business. To achieve this goal, Halliburton is primarily relying on communities of practice, using best practices discovered through prior APQC research. Launching eight communities of practice in 2002, Halliburton achieved a documented 50 percent return of investment in the first year. Gains are continuing to mount, and more communities are launching each quarter.

IBM: leveraging for revenue growth—IBM is the world's leading provider of computer hardware. The company's service arm is the largest in the world and is also one of the largest producers of both software and semiconductors. When Lou Gerstner took over as chairman of IBM in the 1990s, he stated in the annual report that the organization would be the premier knowledge company in the world. For IBM, knowledge management was necessary to its business model, which focused on services in addition to IBM's mainstay in hardware systems. So IBM moved away from hardware and into solutions and services as the primary model. Services required a greater reuse of knowledge about successful solutions, reuse of expertise, proposals, and service delivery models. IBM's information management systems were joined by knowledge management as a key component of IBM's ability to deliver on its promise to shareholders. Knowledge management at IBM supports its five overarching strategies.

1. **Grow the business base**—increase revenue, win rates, and market share.
2. **Manage profitability**—increase productivity and time savings, which can drive profitability, and reuse to enable value pricing.
3. **Set the industry bar for quality**—Produce higher-quality deliverables and generate increased customer satisfaction with reduced project skills.
4. **Compete based on competencies**—Share knowledge, experiences, lessons learned, and manage intellectual capital effectively so that practitioners have access to the best intellectual capital.
5. **Develop brand leadership**—Increase customer satisfaction and loyalty.

A key factor for executives to remember is that KM initiative objectives are specifically focused on the objectives of their organization and not just loosely linked to strategy. During the benchmarking study *Successfully Implementing Knowledge Management*, we asked the best-practice partners to provide the identified objectives for developing a business case for their KM initiatives. Answers included:

- reuse of past designs and experiences,
- improved quality of products and services,
- building on lessons leaned and shortening the learning curve,
- increased profitability,
- lower operating costs,
- improved quality of products and services, and
- innovation.

In support of an existing strategy, knowledge management efforts have definite goals. I've found knowledge management tied to numerous strategies in the organizations that APQC has benchmarked. As subject matter expert for the study *Measuring the Impact of Knowledge Management*, I saw that, among the best-practice partners being benchmarked, knowledge management's biggest impact was the gain in productivity, followed by capturing and retaining at-risk knowledge.

The business strategy that knowledge management supports will help to determine the best knowledge management tools to use. In *Measuring the Impact of Knowledge Management*, facilitated best practices transfer was reported to have the most consistent impact on productivity and was primarily deployed through communities of practice. A summary of which knowledge management activities had the greatest impact on functional units follows.

- **For operations**—Facilitated best practices transfer is the strongest consistent contributor to productivity and quality and effectively prevents redundancy and reinvention. In operations among the best-practice organizations, facilitated best practices transfer (deployed through communities of practice) was reported to be most effective in building a knowledge-sharing culture and enhancing employee learning, proficiency, and professional development. Operations found After-Action Reviews particularly helpful in avoiding redundancy and retaining at-risk knowledge. Content management systems help avoid redundancy and reinvention, as well as capture and retain at-risk knowledge.

- **For sales**—Communities of practice have the strongest impact on improving customer service and building a knowledge-sharing culture, but only have a moderate reported impact on quantitative outcomes because of their wide-ranging activities. Facilitated best practices transfer is sometimes a major contributor to sales growth, as well as learning and professional development. Additionally, expertise locator systems may allow a sales team to differentiate itself from competitors.

- **For research and development**—Facilitated best practices transfer, once again, has the strongest perceived impact on objectives for increasing innovation, avoiding redundancy, and enhancing learning and professional development. Lessons learned and After-Action Reviews have a moderately high impact on all the objectives in research and development. These two approaches are often part of a larger work flow process, such as project management.

Framing the Business Case

Because knowledge management has entered the mainstream of management practices, KM investments must satisfy the same business case requirements of every other investment. When I started studying knowledge management in its early stages, a program might be launched and funded on vision and promise. But in a climate of ever-increasing emphasis on productivity and effectiveness, knowledge management is not exempt from scrutiny.

Both for the initial investment and any expansion effort, you should expect a solid business case from the KM core group, with hard and soft measures of progress and returns. Before a knowledge management initiative is launched, the initial case will be made based on evidence of support for the strategic issue identified in the preceding section. The strategic rationale continues to be important, but offering data to validate the actual impact is necessary to continue financial support. The KM core group should be able to answer these questions: How will knowledge management drive mission and business objectives? What results should we expect? What will be different than today? And how much will it cost?

To provide the necessary evidence for the business case, the KM core group has to be involved in measuring and reporting. (How to measure results will be covered in the next section.) Only in response to solid results can senior managers viably provide and then increase funding, expand programs, or charge business units with gradually assuming a greater share of the responsibility and costs for funding and staffing knowledge management activities.

APQC recently found that many leading knowledge management organizations make their business case based on the subset of measures clearly associated with cost savings or revenue generation and use areas that are intangible or more difficult to measure as significant correlates that come with financial benefit. For example, for Ken Derr, retired chairman of Chevron, making money even when volatile oil prices were down meant significant cost reduction. One of the sources for cost reduction was leveraging best practices and learning faster from experience. Early returns from refineries' sharing best practices, along with results from communities of practices, contributed to the elimination of $2 billion USD in annual operating costs.

A special note is that KM core groups sometimes underestimate the costs for development, maintenance (both business and IT), data purchases, and enhancements. The greatest influence on cost changes for development is evolving changes in the IT requirements. All IT systems require maintenance, enhancements, and staff support. It is especially important that the KM core group has adequately assessed the organization's current IT capabilities to ensure that knowledge management support costs are realistic. (See more in Chapter 3.)

You may want to ask yourself if the business case answers the following questions for you:

- What are you trying to accomplish for your customer?
- Does the business case identify the primary business strategy or strategies it will support? Does it detail how?
- What kind of outcomes should be expected based on supporting this strategy?
- Does the case identify which areas will experience the maximum impact from the initiative?

- Does the business case clearly spell out who will be financially responsible for each component of the project during the next several years?
- Are there proper budget allocations requested for both annual and long-term budgets?
- Is there a schedule of at least annual reviews of ROI and other measures?
- Are sources of internal knowledge identified?
- How will knowledge be captured and transferred?
- What personnel commitment will be required for knowledge management support systems?
- Will the KM core group or business units measure progress and results?
- Are there measures clearly associated with cost savings or revenue generation?
- Will there be multiple channels for knowledge transfer?
- What policy changes will be required?
- Does the implementation plan take into account the unique issues of various business units?
- How will different forms of innovation be tracked?
- Is there a formal communications plan?
- Has the implementation plan been developed with stages one through five in mind?
- Will the initiative survive if a particular individual leaves the organization?
- How will knowledge sharers be recognized and rewarded?
- How will knowledge-sharing behaviors be encouraged?
- What current barriers to sharing knowledge will need to be broken down?

These questions demand a lot of the KM core group but will ensure a successful start to the knowledge management initiative. Otherwise, small setbacks and failures due to inadequate planning could undermine support for the initiative throughout the organization. An area the KM core group will most likely need guidance on in developing the business case is measurement.

To determine what business strategy knowledge management might support, use the APQC KM Measurement Alignment Model™ (*Figure 4*). The model is based on a simple four-step methodology. The steps follow.

APQC KM Measurment Alignment Model™

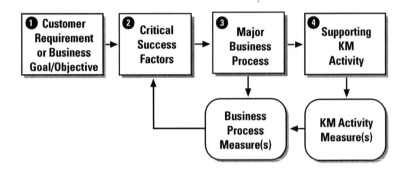

Figure 4

1. Define customer requirements or business goals/objectives. Each organization must have a strategic starting point, which is usually embodied in the business goals/objectives or strategic level customer requirements.
2. Determine critical success factors, which are those key activities or items that must be performed to ensure success. These factors act as necessary, but not sufficient, conditions for success. Individually they will not guarantee success; but without them, knowledge management practitioners will not be successful.
3. Determine major business processes and agree on the one to two major business processes that have a profound impact on meeting the critical success factor requirements. List and define the measures that clearly track process performance in support of achieving the critical success factors.
4. Determine the knowledge management activities required to support the major business processes. Define the knowledge management activity measures that have an impact on the identified business processes.

Gauging Results Through Tangible and Intangible Measures

IBM's KM core group defines measures during the knowledge management initiative design or development phase. The group often selects certain measures because they can be measured. IBM's KM core group follows these eight steps to measure the value of its KM initiatives and initiatives.

1. Determine business objectives and strategy and how the knowledge management initiative will help to achieve those goals.
2. Determine the purpose of the knowledge management solutions to be implemented.
3. Determine who will use measures and how they will be used.
4. Determine which measurement framework is best.
5. Determine what should be measured.
6. Determine how the measures will be collected and analyzed.
7. Determine what can be learned from the measures and what actions should be taken.
8. Revisit the business objectives and align measurements.

At IBM, business unit knowledge management initiatives begin by focusing on efficiency and then evolve to support competency growth in employees, then to speed of responsiveness, and finally to innovation. These measures reflect the maturity of the knowledge management initiative.

The discipline of knowledge management has evolved rapidly through practice. As the processes, tools, and adoption of knowledge management continue to expand, senior managers are rightly asking: "What investments are we making in knowledge management? Are they enough? Too much? What are we getting for our money? What outcomes are we achieving, and what could we expect if we invest more?"

These questions show that measurement is not just a reassuring indicator. Rather, measuring helps ensure that knowledge management initiatives focus on what matters.

Both hard and soft measures are useful to various knowledge management players throughout your organization. Whereas hard-dollar measures include cost reduction, quality improvement, productivity, and increase in sales, soft-dollar measures include cost avoidance, customer satisfaction, cycle-time reduction, quick problem resolution, professional development, and morale. Impact measures should be tied to the business and are often collected through enterprise systems.

Softer measures, more useful than hard measures to knowledge management practitioners and others involved in the actual activities, include trust, good relationships, and indicators of how the process is working. Most measures collected and reported for knowledge management activities are process measures. (These are generally measured monthly.) Process measures help the people in the community or knowledge management activity improve their work; the audience for these measures tends to be the actual people doing the work.

Even though senior managers are compelled to focus on harder measures, having multiple approaches to measurement allows the KM core group to illustrate the value of knowledge management to all the various stakeholders. Executives' drive for hard or quantitative measures has three results. First, it tends to lead to more aggressive measurement practices, such as creating real-time reporting mechanisms. The second result is increased involvement from business units in knowledge management and funding. Third, the entire KM core group becomes actively involved in the measurement process, especially in calculating and reporting benefits.

For example, Ford has identified more than 200 ways of measuring improvement to the businesses, but only 20 of those are in hard dollars. Dollar savings are reported because these are what interest management. Operations, specifically, cares about hard dollars. For the operations and executive audiences, Ford captures hard-dollar savings from energy savings, labor savings, and scrap reductions. Communities show enough hard dollar savings to keep management interested. The most visible gains have been in manufacturing. Ford has seen $300 million USD a year in captured savings during banner years and now average $100 million a year, as reported in 2003. This has totaled $1.37 billion USD since best practices reporting began.

Ford's communities, however, also measure value in terms relevant to them. Each community of practice measures its value in its own metrics. Softer measures include enhanced innovation, as well as improved morale, knowledge retention, employee satisfaction with the work environment, and skills and competencies. Ford noted that a lot of relationships and trust are being built with these softer measures. The financial impact of soft measures and intangibles take more effort to calculate, so measurements are likely to be incomplete. Interpretation, extrapolation, or correlation may also be needed when talking about softer measures. Softer measures do have an impact, however, because they provide a human view.

The effective use of knowledge management measures has the following six characteristics:

1. **Measures are appropriate to a particular knowledge management approach and its objectives.** An organization with a knowledge management approach primarily focused on communities of practice would measure the costs and impact differently than one focused on using a content management system. A knowledge management initiative focused on improving sales force effectiveness would measure proposals and sales. Such measures would be irrelevant to a knowledge management initiative focused on building new knowledge in an engineering discipline.

2. **The organization's measures of success are the starting point.** As detailed at the beginning of this chapter, do not create separate knowledge management measures of outcomes. Instead, use the business measures of outcomes and then work backward to design knowledge management activities and measures that focus on those outcomes.

3. **Extrapolation of gains or savings is done conservatively.** Focus on calculating and reporting the improvements in output measures (e.g., productivity, cost reduction, and quality improvement). Many additional factors affect the ultimate outcomes, such as

overall unit profitability or time-to-market for new products. The dollar value of other results—such as cost avoidance, customer satisfaction, cycle-time reduction, quick problem resolution, and professional development and morale—can also be calculated, but the effort is greater. Although the business case uses all these factors, select the more tangible calculations to capture gains. These alone are often sufficient to justify the cost of the program. The easiest measures to attain come from the process itself and IT applications. These process measures are surrogates for participation and support, not for value. The second easiest measures to capture are surveys of the participants and executives. Extrapolate such gains or savings figures conservatively, partially because they are hypothetical and partially because the number may be well beyond the organization's expectations. Time savings, for example, must be extrapolated conservatively because the resulting numbers in a 350,000-person organization will be so large as to lose credibility. Additionally, with salaries, potential labor savings are only valuable if the time is spent more profitably.

4. **Measures evolve with the evolution of the knowledge management initiative.** Following the stages of implementation in APQC's Road Map to Knowledge Management Results, KM measures evolve with the maturity of the initiative. In the initial stages, measures such as participation and evidence of acceptance matter a great deal. Later, business impact measures grow in importance. Although KM-specific measures are critical to the KM core group and activity leaders, tangible business impact becomes the more compelling evidence for further funding and expansion. When fully institutionalized, a particular set of knowledge management behaviors may no longer be as rigorously measured.

5. **Not all activities need to be measured.** Acting without planning can be expensive. It is important that measures and metrics are developed and collected for the purposes of continuous improvement of the knowledge management initiative. If data is collected just because it can be (by automated methods, for example), then the data could be less than useful, and stakeholders could soon be overwhelmed or unimpressed.

6. **Measurement is kept simple (and successful).** Measures that are difficult to produce or use will cause frustration and quickly be discarded (or ignored). Similarly, the technology to collect the metrics must be easy to use. Just as with the measures, if people do not understand the data collection tools, then the tools will be ignored or discarded. A good measure is one where everyone—whether customer, supplier, or user—understands and uses a standard definition of the measure.

Developing a Measurement Approach

The first key element is to determine a shared definition among groups using each measure. Although each group may use the metric data in different ways, the metric should be calculated consistently. Using the language of the organization (e.g., introducing "employee collaboration" instead of "knowledge management") helps convey the metrics better.

The second key is to determine a standard. For measurement activity to drive performance improvement, an achievable standard must be set for process or activity performance. A standard is defined as the lowest level of acceptable performance. Without an established and communicated standard, the lowest current performance is the generally accepted default standard for an organization.

The third key is to collect and analyze the data for current performance and improvement opportunities in a consistent manner that ensures the reliability and integrity of the data collected.

The fourth key is to report metric data to the individuals and units that will make use of the metric data in decision making. The metric data must be reported in a timely manner so that it can be exploited to its fullest benefit.

The final key is to take action. Once the metric data has been reported, it becomes the responsibility of the owner of the process to take whatever action is required to correct any substandard performance within the process or knowledge management activity.

Metrics to Consider

The metrics listed here are those found useful at Buckman Laboratories, plus some that I think would be useful in tracking the process of building a knowledge-driven organization. You can doubtless think of others, but these will give you a good start at understanding what is happening with your organization over time as you develop and execute your strategy. The key element in all cases is the effort to measure outcomes rather than activity. Metrics include:

- cost per unit,
- customer retention rates,
- cycle times,
- first-contact resolution for customer representatives,
- professional development of your people,
- manufacturing innovation,
- marketing innovation,
- new product sales as a percentage of total sales,
- number of calls handled per day,
- number of defects,
- number of successful launches each year,
- percentage of revenue from new product development,
- productivity,
- revenue from existing customers,
- safety records,
- speed of innovation,
- speed of response to customer needs and opportunities, and
- time-to-market cycles.

Senior managers should never overlook that employees affected by the knowledge management initiative (this should be everybody) will want to be informed about how efforts are progressing and developments in the ultimate business strategy it is supporting. Executives cannot communicate too often, as will be discussed in Chapter 4.

In APQC's benchmarking study *Measuring the Impact of Knowledge Management*, we found that although all of the study's best-practice partners had a tailored blend of measures and methods for knowledge management, they were all able to demonstrate the link among investments, KM activities and behaviors, and desired organization outcomes. Most importantly, partners were able to measure the link to outcomes. Some organizations only measure investments and activities—and not outcomes—because they do not use a framework to develop measures at the beginning of knowledge management initiatives and are not clear about the specific business objectives to be achieved. This relative "fuzziness" may lead to knowledge management activities that are not as crisply designed or deployed as they might be.

Overwhelmingly, the message imparted by the best-practice partners that APQC benchmarks is to measure what matters. If what is being measured does not link to a business strategy or objective or if it does not serve as a leading indicator of future results, then time should not be spent on measuring it.

What Is This Going to Cost?

If you have a dollar to spend on knowledge management, go for connection instead of capture. It's a dollar better spent. [Having] more ways people can talk, more ways people can connect—and that means knowing who to talk to and connect with—is probably the best enabler.
— Larry Prusak, then-senior director for the IBM Consulting Group, speaking at APQC's conference *Knowledge Management: Lessons from the Leading Edge.*

There are costs associated with sharing knowledge. Let's discuss what sort of numbers you are going to see in the business case. In addition to reallocating or hiring employees to initiate/support knowledge management activities, this effort will need funding.

In the benchmarking reports *Successfully Implementing Knowledge Management* and *Measuring the Impact of Knowledge Management,* we asked the best-practice organizations being studied about their start-up costs, as well as annual maintenance and ongoing support costs. The large majority initially spent more than $1 million USD to implement a knowledge program, and the same majority spent the same amount annually.

Of course, the amount is scaled by the size of the organization, but one thing is for certain: knowledge management budgets need to be substantial in the reallocation of time and money (or new money). Do not allow the KM core group to underestimate the time and resources required. Inadequate resources for any initiative can mean an early death and, for knowledge management, can signify to the general work force that the senior leaders are not fully invested, in any respect, in the effort. Although executives are tasked with reviewing and approving resource requests, it is important to empower the KM core group to leverage investments in infrastructure, processes, and people.

Funding models vary from organization to organization, but as with most elements of knowledge management, the true learning organizations have some commonalities. First of all, among those organizations with significant gains in their knowledge management initiative, the funding is higher from the inception of the knowledge management initiative. Also, the cost of the KM core group is less than one-third of the total knowledge management initiative's costs. Finally, over time, costs shift from the organization's budget to the business units'.

In the 2003 benchmarking report *Measuring the Impact of Knowledge Management*, the best-practice organizations' median annual cost per participant was $152 USD, and the median impact was $337 per participating employee. This is a significant ROI, because most of these organizations had thousands of employees participating. The size of the investments varied widely, ranging from $1 million to $100 million annually, depending on the objectives, scale, and scope of the knowledge management initiative and how integral the activities were to the core business process. The annual impact of their KM initiatives ranged from $7 million to $200 million, with a median impact of $15 million. All of the organizations reported continued investment in and expansion of the initiative. (These organizations are now experiencing an increase in direct labor and participation costs, which one would expect if the knowledge management initiative is expanding. However, even though participation is rising, travel costs are down because more work is being done virtually.)

The significant ROI found in this study was not necessarily a function of maturity or length of time managing knowledge. The best-practice distinction is focusing knowledge management initiatives on business objectives and measuring the tangible outcomes. As with APQC's other knowledge management consortium benchmarking studies, the 2003 study found that the leading organizations' KM core groups answer to both corporate and the business units for funding. When a knowledge management activity is clearly proven useful, the business units begin to pay a larger percentage, either through direct labor or allocated charges. The business unit is then accountable for sustaining the knowledge management activity. Typically, business units then pay for time and staff. The KM core group continues to provide strategy, coordination, and tools and is involved in measuring. As new knowledge management activities are launched, the KM core group tends to underwrite the initial cost, and the shift begins again.

Because the organizations studied have business units involved in funding approval, there was accountability to the business units for relevant results. Ensuring the functionality and day-to-day usefulness of the knowledge management activities becomes key because it is the users of the activity—the business units—who approve its continued funding. Business units have very clear priorities. They want to know how knowledge management is going to solve whatever problems are keeping them from reaching their own goals. If knowledge management has truly been aligned with key business strategies, then this should be no problem.

Up to this point, the book has explored elements of a KM initiative that executives are traditionally involved in, to some degree. A key differentiator for best-practice organizations is that senior managers maintain a presence through the additional stages of implementation. This will include overseeing the creation of technology support, culture, and communications. Let's examine executives' role in each critical success factor.

Technology Support Structure

Knowledge management is not just the technology. But it still is important.

It is no coincidence the information technology for easily connecting people and information blossomed at the same time that knowledge became recognized as the most valuable of an organization's assets. There is a powerful symbiotic relationship between knowledge management and IT that is driving improved returns and increasing sophistication on both fronts.

Just a handful of years ago, technology was touted for its ability to put any information you need in your hands. Now technology is tasked with helping shield employees from "information overload," as productivity is threatened by too much information and not enough relevant knowledge.

Every executive is familiar with being overwhelmed by the data, information, and knowledge available. An intranet search can return hundreds of matches. We rely on technology not just to retrieve information, but also to rate it for relevancy, timeliness, and validity. Sometimes, it is not a Web page, but a real, live expert you need. How do you quickly find one? Furthermore, units and communities of practice create and manage their documents in idiosyncratic ways that are understandable to their members but not accessible to the rest of the organization without "the code." And there are also security issues surrounding making information available. These are all knowledge management issues. They are also all technology issues.

The key is selecting solutions that bring technology into the way the organization already works, with a single, common infrastructure and a single, consistent interface. This may include the Internet, e-mail/messaging, groupware and collaboration systems, repositories, indexing, wireless technology, video/teleconferencing, content management systems, portals, or search engines and expertise locator systems.

The availability of new technologies, particularly the Internet, has been instrumental in catalyzing the KM movement. Information technology, if well-resourced and well-implemented, may provide a comprehensive knowledge base that is quickly accessed, interactive, and of immediate value to the user. However, there are many examples of systems that are neither quick and easy to use nor problem free. The development of tools that support easy knowledge sharing, particularly in organization-wide KM programs, is not a trivial task.

The importance of making connections—of people to people and people to information—is the driver to use IT in KM initiatives. Some basic tenets should underline how IT supports a KM initiative.

1. IT is helping to build KM into work processes, so IT and KM staff need to work together. IT and KM staff should be involved throughout the implementation stages.

2. Like all knowledge-sharing practices, try to embed the IT tools into processes that will help employees achieve their work objectives. Instead of adding responsibilities, technology should make a person's day easier.

3. IT for KM has become affordable for most organizations, but there are hidden costs. Technology costs may be the most obvious. (Just double what the vendor quotes you.) The bigger costs are associated with the people who add value to the information, make it accessible to others, and help others find what they need. The hidden costs are in the people, but so are the returns.

4. Common standards for technology architecture are critical for widespread access and use. The typical architecture is based on corporate intranets and Web-based technologies supported by collaborative groupware and database application. Essentially, most of the basic IT infrastructure is likely already in place at any established organization. Integration and scalability are issues that the KM core group should address with the CIO in KM's business case for enterprise-wide implementation.

This chapter will briefly discuss some of the most popular tools in the intersection of knowledge management and technology: portals, content management systems, expertise locator systems, and virtual collaboration. None of these tools demand that senior management has a high level of technical expertise concerning development. However, these tools have a potentially significant variability in breadth of scope, and senior management will be tasked with setting guidelines around these tools to ensure the technology truly supports the purpose of the knowledge management initiative.

Portals

As we all know, the Internet is now the primary vehicle for explicit information flows. The development of browser-based interfaces and client tools constitutes incremental improvements to old technologies, yet their potential impact cannot be overstated. When coupled with rapid increases in bandwidth availability, these developments present an enormous opportunity to reach many people with content they need. In the new Web-based global business environment, an organization can render sophisticated, browser-enabled applications, or portals, to market to target audiences (internal or external) without the impediments of capital-intensive infrastructure and expensive support personnel. These portals can even be "rented," or "hosted," on a subscription basis (i.e., per user or per month) from a hosting provider, which can dramatically improve the current value proposition.

Organizations adopt different approaches to addressing the opportunity customer and supplier portals. Others have a more immediate need to deal with their suppliers and customers and start with outward-facing portals. In both cases, more often than not, the repositories of information and content are kept separate, thus perpetuating a difficult situation. There are a plethora of companies that still have multiple databases of records for their customers.

The key is to focus on the objective of the portal and the nature of the information available, be it procedural information, a lessons learned database, communities of practice sites, and/or e-mail. Like all IT initiatives, senior managers need to be firm in establishing a cut-off date when no new IT requirements will be considered for the initial rollout of the project. Database suppliers routinely charge extra for network versions of their products and usually charge additional fees as the number of either locations or users increase. Software license purchases and annual software maintenance fees are frequently neglected in budget planning. Training and travel expenses, as well as any costs for training materials preparation, must be carefully calculated. IT hardware purchase, depreciation, and maintenance costs at all remote locations need careful evaluation. All central IT costs for support must also be calculated and agreed on by the CIO before development begins.

Content Management Systems

Content management systems provide meaningful and timely information to end users by creating processes that identify, collect, categorize, and refresh content using a common taxonomy across the organization. A content management system (CMS) includes people, processes, and technology.

It is important not to underestimate the potential problems in content management and the resources required to determine your organization's exact needs and capabilities. Content management technology and work flows support a digital publishing process; when they are good, they eliminate online publishing bottlenecks and optimize the reuse of media and content. From a knowledge management perspective, the real question for content managers is not "What content do I have?" but "What content do I need?" Managers must then ask, "What is the best way to get it?" Only when these questions are answered does it makes sense to find technology to enable the digital flow.

Content can include databases, documents, presentations, or e-mail—that is, virtually any artifact of transactions or dialogue or creative work, inside or outside the organization. Content is more than just documents or presentations; it also includes audio clips, streaming video files, and animated graphics. Increasingly, content management includes external content (news feeds, subscriptions to data and analysis, and publications) and content from the extended enterprise (suppliers, customers, vendors, consultants, and external sales). As explained in Chapter 1, users want to be able to access internal and external content from the same system and with the same queries, and they want to know if content is useful and trustworthy.

In an ideal world, a content management system should be the nerve center for the enterprise information infrastructure by coordinating the creation and acquisition, management, delivery, and expiration of content across all business systems. As an aggregator, the CMS technology should piece together content from disparate systems and applications into meaningful artifacts based on unique requests. The content management system should also manage the content from these systems and applications, assemble it based on the needs of the content recipient, and publish the information in whatever format is required.

This is the ideal world; the reality is that most organizations have a wealth of information in a variety of repositories ranging from databases to file servers to individual laptops, which are owned and managed by a variety of functions for a variety of purposes. Just plugging in a technology solution is unrealistic. The needs of the content recipient can only be addressed through a systems approach.

Ultimately, the content management system should:

- streamline the process to capture, classify, and disseminate content;
- provide easier, faster access to information;
- increase productivity of knowledge work;
- standardize technologies for managing content across the organization; and
- improve decision making.

Business cases often offset the initial request for funding on the basis of cost reduction and productivity improvement, even though there should be a more strategic rationale for the system. There are three potential bases for making the initial business case for a content management system:

1. the opportunity to reduce costs and/or increase productivity as the organization conducts its work,
2. the opportunity to manage and deliver content more effectively so that the mission of the organization does not suffer, and

3. the opportunity to increase the revenue stream through the better support for sales and marketing by enabling customers to find content they need and want or by selling content to customers.

The initial investment in content management systems varies from modest (less than $500,000 USD) to several million dollars. The primary cost driver is labor for design, development, and implementation, rather than software and systems. Design elements include:

- background and strategic context;
- evidence of need;
- potential benefits, outcomes, and indicators of success;
- organizational accountability for planning and design;
- initial investment requested;
- resources and their source;
- process for evaluating technology; and
- project plans, including next steps, timeline, and deliverables.

Many of the early adopters of content management systems developed their own content management applications and are now moving to commercial applications, which will require further investment. Organizations provide significant support resources in order to design content management systems and customize information technology applications. The central IT function typically funds the infrastructure, development, software, and maintenance. Business units typically underwrite the costs for ongoing content management activities. If technology must be purchased, then assess the costs required to acquire, customize, support, and implement an application. To get an estimate of overall costs, include the people costs involved in gathering the data, auditing the data, and supporting the users.

Common measures of success include: process improvement functions such as a defined work flow, system traffic, labor costs and cost reduction, quality of content, and customer and user satisfaction.

What makes a content management initiative successful is not only the strength of its central support structure, but also the depth and breadth of its decentralized support structure. For the content management system and the changes associated with it to permeate into employees' daily work habits, there needs to be local support and leadership in the business or functional units in the organization. Budget responsibilities for the following functions are typically centralized in a content management initiative:

- **strategy and process redesign** (to ensure that the initiative aligns with strategy),
- **infrastructure and central support** (to leverage existing functionalities and be in sync with the rest of the organization),
- **specialized services such as taxonomy creation and information categorization** (to create one overarching taxonomy for the company), and
- **communications** (to maintain corporate identity standards and communicate organizational standards).

The following are typically decentralized budget activities:

- **content creation and validation** (Created at the business unit level, content creation is part of an employee's job and is funded by the business.),
- **technical support for content management systems after deployment**, and
- **business unit-specific communications**.

The support roles required for a CMS reflect the overall knowledge management initiative: 1) a steering committee; 2) a core group that guides the CMS and creates templates, common frameworks, and guiding principles; and 3) the content managers who reside in the business units where content and knowledge are created and used and who have responsibility for content relevancy and accuracy.

Without centralized budgeting and decision-making responsibilities, content management would not be at the top of the business units' objectives, thus leaving a reduced level of effective implementation models. Corporate-level leadership, vision, and strategic objectives are clearly needed to drive true content management implementations into mainstream business processes and activities.

Expertise Locator System (ELS)

An ELS can help your work force:
* retain valuable knowledge from retiring or exiting colleagues,
* identify colleagues with specific skills needed for specific projects,
* rapidly collaborate,
* identify new ways to coordinate efforts,
* identify appropriate speakers and experts for external relations,
* recognize knowledgeable colleagues,
* identify who may need training, and
* have a central location for a comprehensive "yellow pages."

As organizations become more complex and more globally dispersed and as expertise becomes more specialized, leaders are looking for methods to help employees determine where to search and find answers. An expertise locator system (ELS) is a viable integrated approach to connect people to people, as well as provide support for communities of practice. The main goal is to organize and distribute knowledge of experts, both inside and outside of an organization or business unit. More than querying existing information, colleagues have an opportunity to exchange information that may not have previously been documented.

The term *expertise locator system* is relatively new in the software industry. Employee directories, on the other hand, have been around for a long time. The term *directories* refers to a list of names that contains specific information about an individual, such as his or her title, role, manager, and department. In most organizations, these directories are maintained by human resources personnel to keep a current list of employees at an organization. Some organizations have considerably expanded the use of these directories to list employee skills or interest areas in an effort to promote communication and knowledge sharing among employees. These enhanced directories are the simplest form of expertise locator systems.

There are three types of ELS solutions: packaged, custom, and hybrid. Package solutions, bought off the shelf, have software that may be of better quality and higher integrity than a custom solution.

A custom solution, on the other hand, is built in-house and should do exactly what you want it to do. For a custom solution, there are no licensing costs on an annual basis; however, these costs are typically a wash with costs incurred internally for upgrading the application for new functionality. A hybrid solution can provide a little bit of both benefits: the structure of an existing system and the customization benefits of extending the application.

Often a first concern raised by someone considering an ELS is the potential burden on anyone designated as an expert. After all, experts are in short supply and do not have extra time to answer questions from colleagues in the field. Further, providing answers may not be part of their job responsibilities. As subject matter expert for the 2004 benchmarking study *Expertise Locator Systems: Finding the Answers*, I found that most leading organizations help employees find expertise and knowledge providers while not designating individuals as "experts."

As is the case with the content management system, the ELS should directly support the goals of the knowledge management initiative and the organization's overarching strategic goal. Within that framework, there are three different models for positioning ELS in the organization. Model one, the knowledge provider and seeker model, focuses on connecting people to people. Model two positions the ELS as a way to staff projects and support competency management in the organization. Model three positions ELS in the traditional mode of identifying designated experts.

Ongoing maintenance costs for the ELS are modest by IT standards. ELS requires a relatively small number of IT and knowledge management staff for maintenance.

> *For us, ELS is an integrated system of processes, applications, and content that connects people to people. It allows us to match every customer requirement or future opportunity with the optimum mix of personnel and resources. The tools and practices we've created encourage and enable people to seek, find, and connect with colleagues, peers, and experts beyond their immediate office network, creating, in effect, a virtual resource that spans the entire corporation*
> —Mark Britton, knowledge management project manager for Northrop Grumman Integrated Systems

APQC has benchmarked a number of excellent ELS systems, including the system at Air Products and Chemicals Inc.. The ELS has almost 2,400 active users, of which about 800 are in the R&D organization. ELS is used mostly for technology alerts, but the user base is increasing and expanding to other areas such as communities of practice, sales, marketing, IT, engineering, one-on-one collaboration, and mentoring.

Searching Air Product and Chemicals' ELS for an expert or alert is similar to searching the Internet. The searcher enters one or more search terms with optional Boolean commands. Search results may contain names of experts and profile excerpts or short pieces of an alert. Clicking on the appropriate search result will link the user to either the profile screen or the full alert. Links are available from the profiles to the corporate directory.

Success is not measured for the ELS tool, but rather for the process it seeks to automate (i.e., technology alerting). Recent surveys indicated that nearly 70 percent of users said that alerts caused them to talk with someone else or show the information to someone else. Eighteen percent of users reported that at least half of the alerts they received prompted conversations with others. The actions taken by readers as a result of alerts included addressing competitive threats (30 percent) and calling inventors (10 percent).

Throughout the deployment of its ELS, Air Products and Chemicals has learned many lessons and seeks to leverage them as it continues to upgrade and gather feedback. The team identified four critical success factors.

1. Tie the ELS to an existing business process. In the company, new process initiatives are sometimes perceived negatively. By tying ELS to an existing process seen as valuable by employees, the team immediately generated support for the ELS.
2. Give people a vested interest in posting and maintaining profiles. Collaboration and the opportunity to receive new information on topics of interest is a motivator, and the price of admission is completing and updating a profile.
3. The ELS needs both bottom-up and top-down support to expand throughout the enterprise. The organic growth of the system in its early years built a very strong foundation in a pivotal user group.

However, to gain the credibility and acceptance of the enterprise, more executive support (from the KM core group) was needed.

4. Keep the system low maintenance. The more maintenance costs required for systems, the higher the likelihood it will be a target for budget cuts. Keeping the system simple and easy-to-use not only improves the user experience, but also allows it to "fly under the (budget-cutting) radar."

Virtual Collaboration

Whether due to travel restrictions or geographically dispersed teams and communities, an increasing number of employees are doing an increasing amount of work virtually. With these trends comes the need for effective collaboration across locations, enterprises, and geographies. Collaboration, I've found, is a core value at all of the best-practice knowledge management organizations that APQC has benchmarked. Most people need the ideas of others within and outside their own teams to get their work done. People in these organizations cannot resist a request for help and feel appreciated for sharing ideas and insights.

The evolution of virtual collaboration tools and approaches is allowing organizations to expand beyond the traditional team-based work and project boundaries. As a result, the dependencies are now among people geographically dispersed, but the competitive pressure is to perform as quickly and as well as they did when they were face-to-face most of the time.

As virtual collaboration poses opportunities to save money, improve productivity, and span boundaries, executives are asking a number of questions: Is virtual collaboration more productive? Does virtual collaboration have an impact on effective decision making? What types of processes and structures are required for successful virtual collaboration? Does virtual collaboration have a long-term impact on the organizational culture and leadership?

Collaboration means working together in a joint effort, and *virtual collaboration* means working together in a joint effort, regardless of location and time. Within these two definitions, there are three different degrees of virtual collaboration: communicate, connect, and collaborate. The two primary differentiators for the three degrees of virtual collaboration are the task complexity (routine or not routine) and the interdependencies (i.e., requirements) of interaction.

Both communities and project teams work along this scale. A project team is a group of people who interact through interdependent tasks that are guided by a common purpose or goal and include both project and functional activities. In comparison, a community of practice is a group of people who come together to share a common interest or topic and to learn from one another.

There are a number of tools to support virtual collaboration: e-mail, instant messaging, teleconferences/conference calls, Web conferences, networked computer drives for file sharing, collaborative computer software, the intranet, Internet access, collaboration Web sites or Web-based applications, and video conferencing.

Virtual collaboration is more about change management than about tools or technology. A global network that provides a shared space for people with common goals to work together is just one part of the equation. The network and the collaborative approaches it supports must be tied to overall business goals and objectives.

In the 2004 benchmarking report *Virtual Collaboration: Enabling Teams and Communities of Practice*, APQC reported that organizations with successful virtual collaboration approaches provide guidelines to their teams and communities on how to be effective in a virtual environment. We found that these may include a defined process for requesting virtual collaboration support, dedicated technical resources to provide support for virtual collaboration, and training on collaborative tools.

For the best-practice organizations we have benchmarked, having a defined process and criteria for requesting virtual collaboration support includes assessing the appropriateness and/or readiness of the requesting teams or communities for virtual collaboration. You may need to determine whether groups wishing to collaborate virtually: are aligned with business objectives, have spelled out the complexity of tasks, would benefit from operating on a global scale, and need access to resources outside of their group. In terms of readiness, you may need to request a business case with:

- identified and established roles,
- connectivity for all members,

- identified and addressed change management issues
  (e.g., communication and training),
- training on virtual collaboration tools,
- information management support (e.g., funding, FTEs, and
  infrastructure),
- processes (e.g., taxonomy or document management policy), and
- measures and metrics for success.

Most significant barriers to effective virtual collaboration are human-related and not specific to any tool set. Individuals tend to rely on nonverbal cues such as mannerisms, posture, facial expressions, and environmental factors in daily one-on-one interactions. So this new virtual method of communication does not come naturally. Support and training in the process of collaborating virtually is important to address not only the specific details of a particular virtual collaboration tool set, but also the process of communicating without nonverbal cues.

Even in organizations with liberal controls over their virtual collaboration requirements, the utility of standardization in the virtual collaboration tool portfolio should be recognized and the use of standard tools and best practices should be widely marketed and communicated.

Supporting Your Work Force

For any KM-related technology, necessary support can be segmented into three areas: IT support, communication support, and training. It is important to distinguish between IT support and communication support. IT support is generally technical assistance on the actual software and hardware used. Communication support, on the other hand, is provided in response to the lack of experience and knowledge most users have in the communication and collaborative methods that must be employed, as well as in response to unfamiliar programs. Communication support aims to directly address the common organization of information and the learned behaviors that are required to make knowledge sharing successful. Concerning training, the open sharing of information and documents is a behavior that must be learned. You must do more than provide basic training on the operation of virtual collaboration software; your employees need to understand the rationale behind using these tools and how it enhances efficiency. KM initiatives are more likely to be successful when users are taught how to use the tools and how to work together virtually. Furthermore, training is an opportunity to disseminate best practices and lessons learned.

CHAPTER 4

Culture and Communication Strategy

Changing the culture was very difficult. It required a lot of effort and dedication to make it happen because there were a lot of nonbelievers we had to convince. But the result was absolutely fantastic.

— Saad Bargach, president of drilling and measurements, Schlumberger Oilfield Services, speaking at APQC's conference *Next-generation Knowledge Management*

Like many observers of the knowledge arena, I see the trend of tacit knowledge becoming more important not only as a potential source of explicit knowledge, but also by initiative, enriching, and maintaining corporate culture. ...It's a crucial moment; unless we do it very carefully, we can make a mistake of throwing away the corporate culture, which is really a different word for accumulated wealth of tacit and explicit knowledge in a manner that is very special to your organization.

— Yotaro Kabayashi, chairman of the board, Fuji Xerox Company, speaking at APQC's conference *Next-generation Knowledge Management*.

As you can see by this point in the book, knowledge management is not just about technology. Although sharing knowledge on a large scale is enabled by IT, technology alone does not provide any gains for the organization; the people using that technology to improve a business process create the value. Leveraging knowledge is only possible when people value building on each other's ideas and sharing their own insights. Allow me to restate that successful knowledge sharing should be tightly linked to a pre-existing business strategy. Sharing knowledge simply enables people to pursue that strategy more fully. Because primary strategic issues are likely to be widely recognized throughout the organization, linking knowledge sharing to these core values gives it considerable weight and importance. If the compelling reasons are not present and the culture is not receptive to sharing knowledge, then no technology system will help.

Although it certainly helps to begin your knowledge management initiative with a culture already receptive to learning and sharing, it is not a prerequisite. Culture change is more often a consequence of knowledge sharing than an antecedent to it. You (and not the IT staff) have the influence to cultivate a knowledge-sharing culture throughout the stages of implementation.

This chapter will discuss the dynamics of organizational culture and its relationship to knowledge management and change management. I list questions to ask yourself to determine if your organization is open to sharing and what steps to take so that employees leverage the resources you have provided to share and capitalize on relevant knowledge.

Cultural Dynamics

Relationships and building a sense of community—that's what causes replication. ... If you've got leaders who are visionaries, it's a whole lot easier than if you don't. We have changes in leadership, but you get one that is supportive and you've got to take advantage of that time frame. And if you can get this institutionalized to a cultural stage, then that's the key. Our timing was just fortunate.

—Stan Kwiecien, Best Practice Replication deployment manager, Ford, in a working APQC white paper

In APQC's benchmarking report *Creating a Knowledge-sharing Culture*, the study's subject matter expert, Richard McDermott, made an excellent point: However strong your commitment to knowledge management, your culture is stronger.

The culture is the environment that influences behavior; decision making; and the organization's approach to markets, customers, and suppliers. It is the combination of shared history, expectations, unwritten rules, and social mores that affect behavior throughout the organization. Culture is the underlying beliefs that, although rarely actually articulated, are always present to color the perception of actions and communications. These beliefs are transmitted through everyday language and actions.

Organizations rarely have a monolithic culture: various "micro-cultures" thrive. And like microclimates, these cultures can vary widely. The culture in the sales organization will not be the same as R&D. Values influence employees' perception of knowledge and the extent to which it should be managed. Selecting where to focus knowledge management initiatives to get the greatest value primarily depends on determining where the biggest ROI is; but ignore culture at your peril as you move into change. Different perceptions of the importance of knowledge management principles will lead to conflict and renegade subgroups.

If knowledge is hoarded as power in an organization, then you will see evidence of that in the limited interactions of employees confined to a "need to know" basis. If employees do not trust coworkers or perceive that senior management is trying to capture knowledge in order to prepare for layoffs, then you will see virtually no knowledge transfer or contribution. If employees feel that knowledge should only move through the hierarchical structure or if groups perceive knowledge from other sources to be irrelevant, then you will see no breakdown in organizational barriers. Furthermore, embracing knowledge management principles will be fragmented and short-lived.

To reposition how knowledge is perceived—across the organization—aggressive communications and leading by example definitely influence the norms and behaviors of employees and units.

Is Your Firm Open to Sharing?

Because culture influences any form of change management, the modern executive must carefully assess his or her organization's culture and own influence on that culture. This involves identifying what dynamics will support the change, as well as what barriers can be expected. It can be helpful to have a checklist for executives to pinpoint potential potholes.

- ☒ Are employees receptive to learning opportunities?
- ☒ Does the organization make a point to hire intellectually curious employees?
- ☒ Do employees feel their job is no less secure by sharing information and revealing mistakes made?

☒ Do employees identify more with the company than with their individual professions?

☒ Is the opportunity to explore new and innovative ideas a part of each employee's workday?

☒ Are employees given time to teach each other? Is teaching and mentoring a factor in promotions?

☒ Are settings to identify mistakes and lessons learned separate from individual evaluations?

☒ Do the major work flows through the organization enable employees to frequently interact?

☒ Are problems and opportunities addressed in a collaborative manner?

☒ Do managers encourage and respect different opinions and suggestions for improvements?

☒ Do employees feel as if no business topic is too sensitive to discuss?

☒ Do employees feel that they can approach any level of manager within the organization?

☒ Do business units recognize that relevant information may come from other units and external sources?

☒ Do managers encourage their employees to help employees in other units?

☒ Does senior management understand the reason for differences in values among units and subgroups?

☒ Do employees understand the long-term benefits to sharing what they know?

☒ Are employees who provide innovative ideas recognized or rewarded?

☒ Are employees who collaborate and build off others' ideas recognized or rewarded?

☒ Are team-based performance and accomplishments recognized before individual accomplishments?

A yellow flag should be raised if you cannot answer these questions. Both the KM core group and senior managers should be aware of the organization's current state before establishing the business case (and the extent of the need to change behaviors) for a knowledge management initiative. The KM core group must be able to answer these questions to gauge resistance and make appropriate measures for implementation of the initiative. And the senior leaders must be able to answer these questions to carry out in an informed manner their crucial responsibilities for communications.

An answer of "no" to any of these questions may be the unintentional result of specific policies and management approaches throughout the organization. For instance, why would a work force not be receptive to learning opportunities? Is it because they have pressure to perform on specific goals, without any managerial expectations for professional development? Is individual expertise more valued than assisting or mentoring others? Has the organization failed to provide training opportunities or encourage employees to expand their responsibilities? Does the organization not make a point to hire and promote intellectually curious and sharing people?

This is an excellent place for both executives and the KM core group to review what practices in place will work against the knowledge-sharing behaviors needed during knowledge management implementation. The KM core group may be able to recognize certain barriers, but it will likely be within the executive domain to aggressively eliminate counterproductive policies. This may involve placing "training" on the balanced scorecards for both units and individuals, rewarding collaborative efforts over the "lone hero," directing the organizational development unit to expand employees' learning opportunities and managers' expectations, spelling out for the human resources unit what qualities you want in new employees, and making an example at the top by tying promotions to knowledge-sharing behavior.

A critical aspect is trust. Executives, as well as middle managers, must trust employees to sensibly use available knowledge and empower them to act on that knowledge. Whereas rules and stipulations for decision making may hinder sharing knowledge or innovatively addressing problems, an organization that empowers employees to freely act on knowledge from other areas of the organization will have a work force with a strong sense of ownership and responsibility for the organization's goals.

The Executive's Role in Cultivating a Knowledge-sharing Culture

> *Viewing culture as a knowledge resource suggests a crucial role for senior management in shaping this asset. Given the difficulty in changing culture as well as the far-reaching impacts it may have on the organization, senior management must take the lead in shaping the values, forms, and practices of the firm to enhance the competitive positioning of the firm.*
> — Clyde Holsapple, editor of *Handbook on Knowledge Management*
> (Springer, 2003)

Knowledge management is easier to implement if it starts at the top of the organization; knowledge-sharing begins with a CEO who "walks the talk." In the benchmarking study *Successfully Implementing Knowledge Management*, we found that 70 percent of the study's best-practice organizations report that powerful CEO support most impacts the creation of a knowledge culture. Executives act as the spokespeople for a knowledge management initiative in order to ensure enterprise-wide support and a consistent perception of the importance of managing knowledge. Senior managers are role models for the values and principles that support the development of a learning organization. I have found that the CEO, as well as every other executive at best-practice organizations, regularly reinforces the need the share and leverage knowledge at every opportunity. Supported by a thorough implementation plan, these executives assure employees that the knowledge management initiatives—and the changes in behavior they may require—will make their jobs easier and more productive. They spell out fundamental assumptions, goals, and values. And throughout the KM core group's implementation plan, they will call on senior managers to intervene; this will reinforce that the initiative is truly aligned with the strategic priorities senior managers have made for the organization. It will also be an opportunity to detail to employees how the initiative will provide a competitive advantage in the marketplace.

The most successful executives visit all levels of the company to see how knowledge is shared. At Ford, when executives visit a plant, they want to see not just where best practices have been identified, but more importantly, where the plant has adopted best practices from elsewhere in the company. Consequently, all plant workers feel compelled to engage with other workers and look for opportunities to improve. This is also an excellent opportunity to provide advice directly to knowledge sharers.

Special attention may be needed for middle management. Because knowledge management initiatives empower employees to access information on their own, middle management will need signals that this change will happen—and is not just an empty resolution. Furthermore, middle management can be highly influential in conveying the usefulness and validity of the KM initiative. Executives should work both directly with the work force and through middle management to ensure everyone understands how knowledge management will help them do their jobs better. It is important to cultivate KM leaders at all levels of the organization.

At the best-practice organizations APQC has benchmarked, I have seen negative consequences for people who either hoard knowledge or do not check to see what others have done before developing their own ideas. These consequences can be in the form of a warning from peers (for example, "If you ask a question that is already in the database, you are likely to get flamed") or a limit to a person's career. An unwillingness to share is more than just resistance to a new approach; it is seen as a direct violation of the primary business strategy to which knowledge sharing is linked.

Finally, executives will need to work with the KM core group to ensure that assumptions made in the implementation plan concerning the organizational culture are realistic. Are the team's perceptions in line with your own assessment of the organization's culture? If not, why not?

The consequence of these efforts is employees' desire to be associated with the forthcoming success of the knowledge management initiative. A key element in approaching employees to gain buy-in is to develop a well-thought-out vision that reinforces how the initiative will support the organization's primary business strategies.

Articulating a Vision

All projects benefit from executive support, but I have noticed that the attributes of executives who support knowledge projects are unique. The executives in the organizations APQC has studied made frequent public comments like, "We're in the knowledge business" or "Our intellectual capital is at least as important as our financial capital." They seemed to be more conceptual and have an implicit faith that knowledge management will benefit their organizations.

At the World Bank, for instance, President James D. Wolfensohn acts as the change agent for the organization by raising awareness of the need for knowledge sharing. Wolfensohn first articulated the vision for a "knowledge bank" in 1996, when he announced that knowledge management would be a key strategy for the organization as it dealt with problems in the future. This announcement caused a profound change in the way the World Bank conducted its business. "The World Bank Group's relationships with governments and institutions all over the world and our unique reservoir of development experience across sectors and countries position us to play a leading role in a new knowledge partnership," he said in his annual speech before the finance ministers of some 175 countries that own the World Bank. "To capture this potential we need to invest in the necessary systems, in Washington and worldwide, that will enhance our ability to gather development information and experience and share it with our clients. We need to become in effect, the 'Knowledge Bank.'"

Ken Derr, retired CEO of Chevron, was also a strong spokesperson for knowledge management. The message he delivered to Chevron employees was that Chevron needed to capitalize on what it knows. He would state, "We must build a culture in which best-practice sharing, reporting units working together, and cross-functional teamwork are the norm."

Visions can provide the foundation for the direction of every employee's daily work by providing purpose, prompting changes, and spelling out what the executive expects from the knowledge management effort. The most compelling vision statements articulate the goal of the initiative and how each employee is empowered to use knowledge management principles in their own work environment. A vision is an excellent opportunity to establish a working environment of trust and openness.

I recommend making "knowledge," in some form, explicit in the company's mission and strategy statements. This will influence what knowledge is considered important and whether knowledge is considered an organizational asset rather than an individual possession.

Using Terms to Reflect Your Culture

The Lotus Development Corp., despite its merger with IBM, is still dominated by the casual culture of software development. This informal culture results in informal teaming to create products and tackle projects. The culture at Lotus is also very forgiving. Things are never "finished" at Lotus, so employees can make changes if their first attempts are not perfect.

Knowledge sharing at Lotus is also informal. There is no explicit knowledge management function. However, individual functions possess knowledge teams that coordinate and facilitate knowledge sharing within the function and across the enterprise. Each function has it own approaches to knowledge sharing, although all approaches are based on the same business needs.

Each organization adapts knowledge management terminology to fit its culture, and each has a different purpose for implementing a knowledge management initiative. It is important for executives to establish a collective understanding of the terms and principles of knowledge management. This will ideally set the stage for the entire organization to use a shared vocabulary.

Leading organizations do not necessarily even use the term "knowledge management" to market their programs internally. Instead, they talk about efforts to share and leverage knowledge, which is easier to explain and more tangible. Such organizations have a branded name for the knowledge management efforts, from "collaboration" to "knowledge networks." Consequently, they have successfully marketed knowledge management to the organization and have a significant number of employees involved in their knowledge management initiatives.

In other words, best-practice organizations vary a great deal in the look and feel of their knowledge-sharing efforts. Some talk directly about the importance of sharing knowledge; have official knowledge-sharing events, sponsors, and structures; sanction communities of practice; and conduct internal advertising. Others avoid using the term "knowledge management" or anything else that could convey (or imply) a vendor solution or could invoke a not-invented-here reaction. Some knowledge management champions actively avoid the term *knowledge* and frame their project only in already accepted business terms (for example, "We're going to reduce cycle time by finding new ways to reuse our engineering designs."). Knowledge management champions must address the language issue in a way that fits their culture.

In all cases, the look and feel of the overall approach to knowledge sharing matches the style of the organization as a whole. The degree of formality, structure, physical resources, and language used to describe the effort matches the overall environment of the organization. This is very different from many "change programs" of the past two decades, where the look and feel of the change program itself was laid on top of the corporate culture. Instead, the look and feel of knowledge sharing is being radically adapted to the style of the organization. To encourage people to share, it is far more important to match the overall style of the organization than to explicitly adopt any specific best practice from another organization.

Formal and Informal Communication

If people in positions of powers say that your organization [is a machine], get a different job. A machine does not need knowledge, machine does not need reflection, a machine does not need to learn. It needs just two things: energy and direction. Machines don't need time to reflect; you burn them until they wear out, and then you buy another one. This is the singular worst possible image for an organization that's interested in knowledge.

— Larry Prusak, then-senior director for the IBM Consulting Group, speaking at APQC's conference *Knowledge Management: Lessons from the Leading Edge.*

For any change management challenge, comprehensive communication leads to more effective performance, improved morale, and a universal internal understanding.

At every stage of knowledge management deployment, employees need examples of success so they can justify dedicating their time to leveraging new technology and changing specific behaviors. One effective way to reach out to employees is through stories. Storytelling is a powerful and memorable way to explain how knowledge management outcomes are achieved and to shine a light on the process of knowledge sharing and use. Although anecdotes and stories are not sufficient to establish a solid business case for continued investment in knowledge management, stories illustrating how measurable outcomes were achieved play a central role in explaining how knowledge management works to those unfamiliar with the details of the process.

Other approaches involve training, online advertisements, and just-in-time coaching for knowledge-sharing behaviors (especially community of practice facilitators).

All organizations and executives have their own style of communicating.

Within Boeing Rocketdyne's process organizations, leadership holds responsibility for coordinating and communicating the importance of knowledge sharing. To communicate knowledge management principles beyond a single location, Boeing Rocketdyne uses communications directly from top management and group-level knowledge management thrust activities, presentations at group-level process council meetings, and meeting at all its sites, in addition to fairs and cross-organization teams. This is accomplished through formal internal communications, backed by a willingness to invest money in knowledge management and the explicit inclusion of knowledge management in strategies. Also, leadership is responsible for communicating the need for sharing knowledge and actively participating in knowledge sharing through meetings.

In a second example, because of senior management's vision, a sound strategy, the involvement of stakeholders from the beginning, and the resources available through its KM initiative management office, Best Buy has faced fewer challenges than other organizations less convinced of the business value of knowledge sharing and retention. Even so, retaining focus on knowledge management is a challenge as it becomes more incorporated into the way work is done. Without executive communication, it is easy to "forget the recipe" and for the next generation to think that knowledge sharing will continue without support.

At Buckman Laboratories, shortly after its knowledge network was introduced, then-CEO Robert Buckman engaged in a lengthy electronic debate about the sales compensation system. Salespeople argued online, sometimes directly with Buckman, about the unfairness of the existing bonus system. The cultural message underlying this open exchange was that anything is discussible, which is a norm that builds the trust necessary to support vertical knowledge sharing. When launching a technology support system for the knowledge management initiative, Buckman stated:

"Those of you who have something intelligent to say now have a forum in which to say it. Those of you who will not contribute also will become obvious. If you are not willing to contribute or participate, then you should understand that the many opportunities offered to you in the past will no longer be available."

From Millennium Pharmaceutical's founding, its leadership has continually stressed that its use of knowledge will drive innovation and move the company from primarily a research-based organization to an innovative, technology-driven, and product-based organization. Using knowledge is a key theme in management communications about how to be more efficiently innovative.

To reinforce this message, the rollout of knowledge management projects to support better and faster decision making has been accompanied by specific communication strategies to the stakeholders and those who must use the new tools.

In addition to formal communications, it is wise to establish channels for informal communications, both between executives and employees and between employees and their coworkers. Best-practice organizations are laced with informal human networks that people actively use to find who knows what, get help and advice, learn how to use specialized tools, etc. Because of their informality, few such channels generate organizational knowledge, yet they have some influence in maintaining expertise about topics important to the organization and allow managers to informally encourage those employees they see working together. Generally, people in these networks trust each other and feel obliged to share information and insights. Through these informal channels, individuals receive appreciation from their peers and often form strong personal relationships. The KM core group may not play an active role here, but it can enable these channels to exist in their informal form by lightly authorizing them and giving them a technology tool, information systems, space, library support, time for network coordinators to manage network affairs, or recognition of their contribution.

For the story to have meaningful impact, Stephen Denning, the former program director of knowledge management at the World Bank and corporate storytelling expert, suggested to attendees at an APQC KM conference to take heed of the following points:

- To avoid becoming an artifact, the story must be told, rather than transferred to film or paper.
- The story must be comprehensible and familiar.
- The perspective must be that of a single hero that represents the essential nature of that organization and its business.
- Stories must be true to ensure the storyteller's credibility.
- To have a springboard effect, the story must have a degree of strangeness or incongruity.
- Tell the story as quickly as possible.
- Do not impose a view onto the audience.
- Let go of control, and encourage the audience to share the story.
- The story must be told with conviction.
- Do not expect success with everybody, particularly middle management and accountants.
- The story has to be married to analysis, such as costs and benefits.
- To energize and galvanize an organization into positive action, avoid negative stories.
- Plan on success, and anticipate outcomes.

Providing Rewards and Recognition

In a perfect world, the benefits of accessing and contributing knowledge would be intrinsic. In some organizations, in fact, they are. People who share knowledge are better able to achieve their work objectives, can do their jobs more quickly and thoroughly, and receive recognition from their peers and mentors as key contributors and experts.

Other organizations, however, need to create more structured rewards and recognition systems to encourage their employees to change their behaviors. Whether these rewards are tangible or intangible, they are a means of acknowledging the value of sharing and knowledge, appreciating the contributions people make, and increasing awareness about the importance of not hoarding what you know.

There is a distinction between "recognition" and "rewards." Recognition is visible, public reinforcement to individuals and teams for their contributions and role modeling of knowledge-sharing behavior. Recognition may be at the community, business unit, or enterprise level. It is also highly rewarding psychology. Sometimes recognition is accompanied by tangible rewards. Tangible rewards may include money, promotions, and substantial gifts. Rewards may or may not be public, but they typically reflect exemplary contribution or performance.

The appropriate approach to rewards varies across stages of KM implementation. In early stages, resources and recognition are rewarding; in later stages, it may be necessary to add rewards tied to formal measurement and performance appraisal. Some organizations develop guidelines instead of a corporate-wide approach. I have seen them charter a cross-functional task force of KM, representatives from some business units, human resources, and the organizational development function to develop guidelines and suggestions for all groups to encourage knowledge sharing. This group might also address the question of whether knowledge sharing should be part of a performance appraisal. With equal success, I've also seen organizations that let each department and business create its own approach. In this scenario, the KM core group works with each business unit to develop its own understanding, paradigm, and approaches to recognition and rewards (under guidelines from the KM core group for variation). Either way, the ultimate goal is to reinforce desired behavior with recognition, time, an endorsement, or something else.

For example, American Management Systems (AMS), a business consulting organization, uses a combination of tangible and intangible rewards for participation in its knowledge system. Employees wish to be recognized as internal subject matter experts and therefore strive to make contributions that present a compelling case for their nomination and confirmation as an associate. AMS publicizes the contributions and contributors who are most in demand in an online newsletter and at associate gatherings. The company also hosts a contest through which employees can receive cash awards for showing the value of the knowledge they have leveraged throughout the year.

No matter how your organization chooses to reward and recognize employees for their role in knowledge management, make sure it aligns with and is supported by your culture. If knowledge sharing is not inherently rewarding, celebrated, and supported by the organization, then "token" awards will be viewed as worthless and may actually have a negative effect. Using explicit rewards for specific knowledge contributions is only moderately effective and loses sight of the big picture.

There are two principles to keep in mind. Behavior that is rewarded gets repeated, and people want to be valued for what they know. Best-practice organizations I have researched typically use one or more of the two following classes of approaches to reinforce the discipline of knowledge sharing:

1. **Host visible knowledge-sharing events for stellar "sharers"**—These events tend to reward people directly for contributing and leveraging knowledge. For example, Siemens measures and rewards individuals for participation in ShareNet. Contributors earn ShareNet shares, relative to the quality and reusability of the contribution, which is assessed through a peer rating. Top ShareNet contributors will be rewarded with an invitation to the ShareNet global knowledge-sharing conference.

2. **Embed sharing and leveraging knowledge into work processes**—The best reward should come from the activity itself. After all, an effective knowledge management initiative will make employees' jobs easier. Incentives for participating in a community of practice are:

- being a part of a community of people with similar interests or needs,
- pride of excellence,
- reducing the time that known experts spend answering standard questions,
- expert exchange, and
- having knowledge targets become part of the professional development path.

Best-practice organizations have also found that including individual measures is valuable for focusing and encouraging desired behavior. A majority of organizations with advanced knowledge management initiatives include knowledge sharing in performance management systems for at least some employees. Best-practice organizations do not see reward and recognition as a way to motivate people to share. Instead, they see rewards and recognition as a way to acknowledge the value of sharing knowledge, appreciate the contributions people have made, and increase awareness of the importance of sharing knowledge.

One key factor is adjusting evaluations and performance appraisals to recognize sharing and leveraging knowledge as a key responsibility. This will do much to drive behavior changes, with promotions and raises on the line. Employees should be expected to understand basic knowledge management principles and illustrate how they have contributed and leveraged knowledge.

At Hewlett-Packard Consulting, the Knowledge Masters Award recognizes the employees whose knowledge mastery best exemplifies the culture of balancing innovation with reuse and contributes to significant and measurable business impact. Winners receive company-wide recognition and an all-expense-paid trip or cash award. Hewlett-Packard Consulting has identified that in addition to the award's power to motivate employees, the process of chronicling outstanding practices represented in the winners' stories resulted in capturing information about millions of dollars in cost savings attributable to KM.

Knowledge sharing is also rewarded at Xerox. In communities of practice, being recognized by peers is a measure of success in itself. The author's name is included on published "tips" to create recognition and ownership of the solution. To formalize the recognition process at the individual level, Xerox created a community hall of fame. Individuals are rewarded by product type based on the number of times their tips were used by others in their community. They get both a cash or prize award and a nomination to the hall of fame. At the corporate level, knowledge sharing has now been added as a component of Xerox's prestigious President's Award.

According to representatives at Lotus, the recognition and visibility that come from sharing knowledge are what keep the importance of sharing at the forefront of people's minds. Knowledge management practitioners at Lotus recognize the difficulty of using quantitative measures to encourage knowledge sharing based on experience. Measures based on knowledge quotas have not been successful in the past. For example, the sales unit had a program, "Cash for Wins," to reward sales representatives for sharing stories. This program had $100,000 USD to award but only paid out half of the money and had a participation rate of less than 10 percent. More importantly, the sales representatives who did contribute were the lower performers who wanted to make up for their low sales quotas. Accordingly, although knowledge management practitioners at Lotus still believe in the potential of measurement systems for institutionalizing knowledge-sharing behaviors, they report that the recognition factor outweighs any benefits that having specific measures for knowledge sharing would provide.

When considering how to create a rewarding culture for knowledge sharing, some general principles follow.
1. Time to use and create knowledge has to be recognized and rewarded; if participants feel that they have to "steal" time from the "real" work to do this, then they won't participate in knowledge sharing.
2. Using the knowledge system has to be self-rewarding to the consumer; users have to get something out of it, be it knowledge they need or a sense of status and recognition.

3. Recognition lies in being perceived as an expert by employees and management. Ensure that internal contributors' or experts' names are attached to documents, guidelines, and presentations they created.

4. Create recognition for sharing, transferring, and using knowledge and best practices; you can do this by celebrating best practices success stories and propagating tales of big savings and important contributions.

5. Recognize all parties or units involved: both those who share knowledge and those who receive knowledge. If both ends are not feeling rewarded, then you will not get the results desired.

CHAPTER 5

Examples of KM Efforts

At this point in the book, we have established a number of models and ideals to guide a knowledge management initiative to truly significant gains. A well-thought-out KM core group has developed a tangible business case and an implementation plan to proceed through the five stages. Senior management has been involved throughout the process to ensure that efforts align with strategic priorities and that the KM core group and all knowledge sharers heed common knowledge management critical success factors. All of this effort is to have a successful enterprise-wide knowledge management initiative.

A compelling case for becoming a learning organization can be made by telling stories, so this chapter provides real-world success stories of how knowledge management initiatives have succeeded. Because these are stories for senior management, I detail the happy endings: a validated, positive ROI.

The first example, **Caterpillar**, has become a leading supplier of agricultural equipment and the world's No. 1 maker of earthmoving machinery. Caterpillar operates manufacturing plants on six continents and sells its equipment worldwide via a network of 220 dealers in about 2,700 locations.

Knowledge management, in one form or another, has been going on inside Caterpillar for some time and manifesting itself in such activities and programs as the use of standards, corporate libraries, internal conferences and forums, membership in professional societies, partnerships with universities, and intranet sites. These activities have been used to support the day-to-day operation of the business.

At Caterpillar, knowledge management means providing efficient, reliable, and easy access to knowledge and collaboration with others across the value chain for the purpose of improving performance. Basically, it is learning what you need and when you need it to improve your performance today.

I Did It My Way

When asked what points they would stress, Caterpillar representatives shared the following lessons learned about their online communities of practice:

- **Usability**—If people cannot use the system easily, then they will not use the system at all. This may seem simple, but it is the focus of the KM core group as it supports the organization in the use of the company's "knowledge network."

- **Focus**—The narrower the focus of the community, the higher its chance for success. Focus on communities of strategic business importance, such as knowledge capture from retirees, to the business.

- **Flexibility**—The system must have the ability to be all things for all people. Caterpillar has found that people will use the tools that have value to them and that this value can shift from group to group according to the focus of the community of practice. Therefore, no specific tool use is mandated for users of its network.

- **Immediate results**—Momentum is everything. To help support change management within Caterpillar and its supply chain, communities of practice need to show immediate impact for the user group.

- **Value**—Activities must produce value. Caterpillar monitors each community of practice for use and initiates or disbands communities of practice as the need or value dictates.

Caterpillar University assumed the responsibility for the Knowledge Network in January 2001 and has played a leading role in transforming the network from an information exchange tool for engineers to an Internet-based strategic business asset that captures and effectively leverages knowledge throughout Caterpillar's many enterprises.

By making knowledge sharing, along with leadership and learning culture, a key foundation in its strategy, Caterpillar University supports the key business objectives of the KM program: to improve performance, support a learning culture, and deliver bottom-line results.

KM activities—The Knowledge Network is the centerpiece for knowledge management at Caterpillar and is based on communities of practice that span the entire value chain. The network's innovative design features, coupled with a taxonomy based on business processes, reflect the business environment at Caterpillar and contribute to the successful integration of the Knowledge Network into the operations of business processes and as an aid in decision making. The Knowledge Network has rapidly gained acceptance and has become an integral part of how Caterpillar does business, as confirmed with documented ROI and consistent growth across all user bases.

Communities of practice serve as the main knowledge management activity within Caterpillar. More than 18,000 Caterpillar employees and others have accessed one or more of the 1,900 communities organized around a specific, business-related topic. A community delegate, or manager, oversees the development and maintenance of the community, controls access, and monitors content. Anybody with access to that community may initiate a threaded discussion involving members from around the world. Automatic e-mail updates of new material are sent to community members. The keys to Caterpillar's successful communities are validated knowledge entries, strong community discussions, and focused expertise location.

People post knowledge entries that pertain to a specific work process, tool, problem or solution, quality issue, or other questions. Each entry is available to users, so the community manager validates and approves each piece of information before it is added to the knowledge repository. The number of knowledge entries has grown consistently and has contributed to the development of a deep knowledge base at Caterpillar.

Community discussion bulletin boards enable anyone with access to a community—including outside experts, suppliers, and partners—to post information relevant to the community. People may view these bulletin boards to gain access to required expertise.

Expertise location is a critical part of each community and the Knowledge Network. Each community of practice manager can assign and label experts as they relate to his or her community. Once experts are assigned, they continue with a community until the community manager relieves them of this duty. This approach allows the community of practice manager to maintain control over the quality of the community while providing the deepest possible knowledge base for all users.

The KM core group—The Knowledge Network is part of the technology-enabled learning group in Caterpillar University. The responsibilities of the KM core group are to:

- act as the corporate process owner for knowledge management,
- provide the budget to operate and maintain the network,
- serve as the system owner for the network,
- develop a knowledge management strategy,
- establish new communities,
- prioritize and manage system updates,
- market knowledge sharing internally and externally, and
- deliver system support and training.

The business case—The Knowledge Network started with one intern and a laptop. Early expectations were modest: capture lessons learned and avoid duplication of effort and tests within the Tech Center. Supporters of this effort were not looking for ROI or targets but were hoping people would talk to each other and avoid duplication of effort.

As the Knowledge Network evolved from a communication tool for engineers to a method used to capture and share knowledge throughout the enterprise, the business case has become more formal. Caterpillar University has committed to annual goals for efficiency and growth, and progress toward these goals is reported monthly.

The selling points used to fund KM activities have evolved from the initial business case of improving communication and duplication of effort to now include improved productivity, immediate value for the user, voice of the customer, and a proven ROI.

When Caterpillar University took over KM in 2001, the benefit of an external focus or voice of the customer was not obvious, but it became clear that the payoff was greatest when linking to external customers. As part of the ROI study, the Caterpillar dealer service training community of practice was studied to quantify the link.

Funding—Knowledge sharing and the Knowledge Network are included as part of Caterpillar University's technology-enabled learning budget and are funded with exempt corporate office dollars. The services of the KM core group and the Knowledge Network are not billed to the business units because the identified gain far outweighs the minimal costs of operations.

Measuring KM—Caterpillar's KM measurement philosophy is best described in four components. First, log everything. If the system has the capability to collect data, then collect it. (Caterpillar asserts that you never know when you can go back and use that data to set a baseline.) Second, measure what you value. Moving from general data collection, it is important to actually collect, analyze, and report the data that has significance to the organization. Third, post system metrics in a timely manner so that all users and community managers can see and act on them. Finally, empower community managers with metrics so they can effectively manage the community.

Over time, knowledge management measurement at Caterpillar has evolved as the technology that enables the Knowledge Network system has improved. In the beginning, the system tracked generic system hits and moved to more comprehensive system detail and community manager metrics; the KM core group now tracks system penetration.

Currently used system metrics provide real-time and historical trending data in all aspects of system use. Some of the measures used are the number of: communities, new discussions, knowledge entries, users, users by affiliation, experts, and attachments, as well as the amount of storage space used. The community manager can drill down the metrics that impact his or her community, such as the number of community visits, the number of visits by knowledge entry, who visited, and when they visited.

Results—Caterpillar has controlled costs of the system and, from 2000 to 2003, has invested $2.5 million USD in the operation and expansion of the KM core group and the Knowledge Network.

(This is a relatively very small investment for an organization of this size.) It is expected that this same level of investment will continue in future years, with projected savings from 2003 to 2008 to reach $75 million USD.

Caterpillar commissioned a third-party researcher to examine the impact of its efforts. The ROI study focused on quantifiable return in five specific areas: personal productivity, productivity of others, speed, cost savings, and quality of the product. Personal productivity was defined as the number of hours saved because the Knowledge Network was used. Productivity of others was defined as the number of hours that others saved by the thread initiator's resolving the issue using the Knowledge Network. Speed of problem resolution was defined as benefits produced by accelerating the achievement of the solution using the Knowledge Network. Cost savings was defined as how the use of the Knowledge Network contributed to reducing annualized costs.

The use of the Knowledge Network to improve the quality of the product was documented. For example, a thread initiator was about to upgrade the specifications of a part. He first initiated a discussion on the Knowledge Network and received a wealth of information he would not have otherwise received. He incorporated many of these ideas into the redesign, which significantly improved the quality and customer acceptance of the part. These quality changes (due to use of the Knowledge Network) were conservatively determined to be $780 USD. The thread initiator attributed 100 percent of this value to the Knowledge Network and was 80 percent confident in that estimate.

The benefits attributed through the study to the Knowledge Network are that Caterpillar receives $10 in cost savings for every $1 spent; internally focused communities average $600 in value per discussion; and externally focused communities of practice generally returned five times greater return per discussion.

The departments that have most benefited from using the Knowledge Network to share and leverage knowledge across Caterpillar, according to the results of the ROI study, were Six Sigma, engineering, manufacturing, human resources, information services, and product support/marketing.

The bottom line—The ROI study examined in detail how two network communities of practice (bolted joints and fasteners and Caterpillar dealer service training) delivered bottom-line value to the business. These community members generated a total of $1.5 million USD from using the Knowledge Network, which was largely driven by the benefit of one case. Excluding this one case from the ROI calculation and factoring in the annualized cost of the Knowledge Network resulted in returns of 212 percent and 738 percent, respectively, for the two communities. An additional $275,000 USD in one-time cost avoidance was documented as well.

Intangible benefits included increased customer satisfaction with Caterpillar equipment, strengthened dealer relationships, increased retention of knowledge, improved collaboration skills, expansion of informal networks, and continual learning.

Let's move on to **Ford Motor Company**, which has made incredible productivity gains through the transfer of best practices. With approximately 350,000 employees, Ford operates in more than 200 global markets on six continents. Its licensed, multiple-step knowledge-sharing process, called Best Practice Replication, is a corporate-wide initiative with recognized successes since the mid-1990s. This rigorous, defined, and measurable process establishes how to collect and approve practices that can be disseminated and implemented across the company. The Best Practice Replication process is characterized by three primary activities: capture proven, valued practices; quantify or qualify the value added to the organization; and manage the process using real-time status and reports, policy deployment, and management reviews.

The beginning—During the last major recession in the late 1980s, a general manager of vehicle operations at Ford believed that in order to improve, the company needed to leverage and replicate the lessons of others. He commissioned a team comprised of one person from every plant with the intent of driving productivity improvements based on the proven successes of others. He believed that transferring knowledge in this manner would lead to a better way of doing business.

How to Get the Most from Your Communities of Practice

It is not particularly easy to build and maintain communities in an organization. During the benchmarking study *Building and Sustaining Communities of Practice*, we found that to sustain a community of practice (CoP), senior management is not the most important factor. Management is instrumental in selecting communities, ensuring their link to business opportunities, and providing resources. Once the communities are selected, however, the most critical success factor is the skill of the community leader. Management can hamper or kill a communication strategy, but it cannot make communities thrive. Identified below are some of the most common challenges faced when integrating communities into the business.

- **The CoP must reflect a necessary and natural grouping of people to create and share knowledge.** Because these people often work and report in separate units, boundary-spanning efforts and sponsorship are essential.

- **Supply-driven efforts are rarely successful.** Organizations often try, with little success, to build knowledge collections based on existing materials and without an active community of practitioners contributing to the effort. The CoP needs to contribute and maintain its content, not have the content created for it.

- **For collaboration to thrive, people must see as well as experience the value of interaction.** Community formation requires a lot of face-to-face interaction. Participation itself should be rewarding.

- **Local community knowledge must transcend the local context and personal experience of contributors to become critical knowledge for the global community.** A process for screening and validating "knowledge and best practices" is essential. As a community convenes and discusses issues, it is important to capture the dialogue taking place so that it can be screened, filtered, and validated by subject matter experts before it is provided as "organizational knowledge" to the enterprise.

The larger team divided into teams of four or five, visited each plant for a few weeks, and learned what could be done to help. During this time team members learned that certain process improvements in place in one plant were not necessarily used by others. These improvements, or best practices, were captured and shared with the other plants. This was the genesis of Ford's Best Practice Replication process.

The next phase was to take this knowledge and deploy the team to actually help implement these best practices and at the same time capture the improvements that come with replication. A matrix was maintained to track the value of these replications.

In time the original team evolved into a core group of four people, but the replication process continued. The team continued to capture knowledge in a standard format known as a picture sheet and send it by mail, fax, and eventually e-mail. The team collected feedback and maintained a matrix of which practices had been replicated and their cumulative value.

In 1995, with the advent of the Internet, Best Practice Replication moved online. The first Web-based transactional database and application at Ford enabled automation of the communication. The company's plants had a process and tool to share knowledge and capture its value. By then, after six years, Best Practice Replication had become a proven success with proven results.

KM activities—Ford's KM activities include communities of practice, best practices transfer, lessons learned, content management, and After-Action Reviews.

Ford has a mature community of practice structure. The communities of practice are naturally occurring groups of people who perform similar work and are geographically dispersed. (Teams, however, are not viewed as communities.) Currently, there are more than 50 active communities of practice at Ford. Only 15 are manufacturing related; the rest are located in support areas such as: human resources; material, planning, and logistics; product development; IT; and finance.

In terms of the transfer of best practices, Ford employs a push process with defined roles and responsibilities. Using Best Practice Replication, communities share proven practices that have improved a business process, rather than ideas. These practices are shared through picture sheets, video clips, and documentation.

In addition to the lessons captured in the Best Practice Replication process, a lessons learned repository was created in 1997 at Ford with the intent of allowing anyone to submit or retrieve a lesson learned. A "lesson learned" was not clearly defined, nor was there any governance as to the submissions. Interpretations of lessons learned were entered without any governance, the result being that few could be accurately retrieved. The lessons learned database was deactivated in 2001.

Currently, "powertrain" operations has developed and is expanding a process called the preventive corrective action system, where a lesson learned is defined as a corrective action that has been effectively closed, can be replicated, and is fed back into Ford's quality operating system to ensure permanent change. Like Best Practice Replication, this system has strict roles and responsibilities, the difference being that the knowledge is captured and included in standards and specifications rather than being replicated by a community of practice.

At Ford, content management is a well-defined process for any documentation that is ultimately searchable on its intranet. A strict governance and review process guides anyone who needs to post to the central repository, or enterprise knowledge base. Each posting is reviewed for adherence to the governance guidelines and for possible duplication. Document retention policies apply. Only properly registered documents with appropriate taxonomies are searchable by the corporate search engine. The actual content is the responsibility of the posting organization. There is a charge associated with the posting that in effect funds the enterprise knowledge base content management process. The cost varies with the volume of activity.

After-Action Reviews are routinely held during the course of any major project. For example, the product development function uses the Ford product development system with milestones at key timing dates. The decision to advance to the next milestone requires reflection concerning whether the goals have been met and what went well or what went wrong. Similarly, during the launch of a new or revised product or service, After-Action Reviews are often held daily with a major review (launch critique) after completion of the launch or project. If necessary, lessons learned during this process are brought back into the operating system to ensure change.

The business case—There was no business case needed for the development of Best Practice Replication. Its value and long-term benefits were visualized in the minds of visionary leadership, and the expectations were communicated to those charged with implementation. The value provided year after year (both soft and hard dollars) is compelling to leadership. Enlightened leadership understands the intangible yet valuable benefits of knowledge management. Over the years, the program office has observed the number of communities grow as seasoned managers with community experience move around the organization to areas that do not have communities.

In the case of other knowledge management initiatives, leadership provides the vision, assembles a team to investigate, and provides the budget based on the team's implementation proposal. ROI figures are required to support the decision-making process, but they are not the only factor. A proposal that is short of the ROI hurdle may still be funded. The IT budget has discretionary funding available for future knowledge management initiatives.

Evidence for knowledge management substantiation most often comes from a survey of the potential users with estimates of time saved through the use of knowledge management initiatives as the value. For example, a survey of product development engineers in the late 1990s found that engineers were spending approximately 25 percent of their time looking for information and finding only about 10 percent of what they needed. These survey results served as the genesis for knowledge-based engineering, which in turn made the engineers more productive.

Funding—Aside from the small group in the KM initiative office, there are no positions fully devoted to Best Practice Replication. For the users, it is just another role, a fractional part of their week-to-week efforts. Aside from the budgeting for the database, the Web developer, and program office support, there is no specific funding for knowledge management at Ford, but businesses realize there is value in participation.

Through the 50-plus communities, the program office supports approximately 25 vice presidents' areas. It is recognized that Best Practice Replication adds value to the enterprise and is included as a line item in the annual IT budget. Custom development is charged on a time and materials basis to business partners.

Measuring KM—Ford's KM initiative office does not launch a community of practice if it can not measure improvement. Everybody who does work, regardless of the organization it is in, has to have some metric that indicates how he or she is improving the business. This improvement need not necessarily be demonstrated in dollars. As a matter of fact, Ford's 50-plus communities of practice have collectively identified more than 200 ways of measuring improvement. Fewer than 20 of those are in dollars. Most communities state savings as percentage improved, customer satisfaction indicators, accident rate reduction, and cycle time improvements. The program office knows these could be converted into dollars; however, it concentrates on showing the value to the users in their own metrics. These improvements ultimately cascade and translate as overall improvement to the bottom line.

Some hard-dollar savings are obvious—such as those that come from energy reduction, material savings, labor savings, or throughput increases—and the program office does capture these. With the value of replication in both the soft values and the hard dollars, there is enough bottom-line value to continue pursuing better ways of doing business through the Best Practice Replication process.

Depending on the community, practitioners and users have a variety of ways to express value. For example, an industrial engineer cares about time. Can time be turned into money? Yes. However, the critical metric to engineers is time. Telling engineers how to save three seconds on a repetitive process is meaningful to them. However, telling them how to save $10 per unit is not as meaningful. The point is that each community measures its improvement in its own metrics and in its own language. The practitioners want and need to see value in their own terms.

Each community of practice picks its own measures, and in many cases, these measures are unique to that community of practice. It develops or uses measures applicable to its business. Each community has 15 to 20 measures, a number considered optimal by the KM initiative office. During the process of developing a community of practice, one important step is to determine the measures and metrics. The focal point in each community of practice is responsible for collecting measures. And, in each picture sheet, there is a field to report the value of the improvement. In some communities, it is mandatory to complete this field. Additionally, the recipients of the knowledge have an obligation to provide feedback concerning each practice. If they do not replicate the practice, then they must explain why. If they do replicate it, then they must explain its value to them.

In the case of communities of practice, the measures are important influences in making the decisions to replicate. The replicating site can relate to what the originator saved or improved and can identify benefits. From the viewpoint of a community of practice, if a value is not identified, why bother to measure something? The program office encourages each community to leverage activities it already does for measurement, rather than inventing new things to be measured.

For knowledge management to succeed, there needs to exist trust, relationships, and an indicator of value. What the KM initiative office encourages is a sense of obligation to share something of value, which in this case is a means to improve a day-to-day process. People need to understand and trust the values described by the measures.

Because many measures are specific to a community of practice, generic measures are not included. Metrics tend to be dynamic and evolve as the community of practice matures. In most communities of practice, there are a select few measures that are relevant to the community members. Therefore, determining which ones are the most successful depends on the community.

The stakeholders are the ones who support the Best Practice Replication process. The program office has learned that there needs to be some measure of dollars in each community of practice to satisfy the stakeholders, even if the majority of the real measures may not be fully quantifiable. The stakeholders typically have higher level key indicators. Measures are reported at the plant and executive levels.

For Best Practice Replication, the number of replications is the most valuable measure because senior leadership can recognize whether employees are using the process. Additionally, in the picture sheets, leaders can see both the hard and soft value of the replications.

Results and the bottom line—In banner years, the Best Practice Replication process has delivered approximately $200 million USD in annual value since 1995, and Ford has documented approximately $1 billion USD of hard value from 1995 to 2002.

The KM initiative office finds overall investments difficult to capture because many are localized within divisions, organizations, or departments. However, Best Practice Replication costs no more than $500,000 USD annually to administer and support. The investment required of the community of practice members is their time and travel (which is infrequent). Time involvement is judged to be .5 hours per week for 3,200 active members. This equates to approximately $2.5 million USD annually. In reality, this is a sunk cost because participation is a role, not a position, and is related to an existing job position. Travel and meeting costs are estimated at $500,000 USD annually. These costs are concurrent with other business needs to travel and meet and are not specific to Best Practice Replication.

The effectiveness of Best Practice Replication is measured by the success of the communities of practice and the value that community leaders report. Additionally, using and sharing knowledge shows up on the annual performance reviews for the focal points and gate-keepers within each community. This step was taken to increase the penetration of best practices and further develop the environment to drive participation.

The results of knowledge management activity drive to the bottom line. The program office considers the values reported by Best Practice Replication, in addition to the hard savings, to be a barometer rather than hard savings. Each organization has specific means to officially capture the actual financial impact.

Additionally, in an attempt to link the value of the activity to Ford's performance measurement system, the roles of focal point and gatekeeper are now part of formal job descriptions, so people in those roles are measured against it. Also, communities are part of manufacturing's balanced scorecard.

Although Best Practice Replication was developed and is used primarily to drive improvement in manufacturing and business support activities, one of the most significant improvements has been in the safety of Ford's employees with a derivative called global preliminary incident reporting. This derivative captures the details of incidents, accidents, and near misses. The Best Practice Replication process immediately communicates these to the more than 700 safety engineers globally as an alert to be aware of any conditions that led to the incident or near miss. A subset of these becomes an immediate corrective action, where the safety engineers are required to confirm compliance to the actions described.

In 1998 Ford's Occupational Health and Safety office measured that for every 200,000 hours worked there was an average of 7.4 accidents that resulted in lost time. In 2002 the average was 1.9 accidents. This is a significant benefit measurable by a very specific industry-wide metric. Use of Best Practice Replication was not the sole reason for improvement, but it was certainly an enabler and contributor through awareness and replication of corrective actions.

Now let's examine a relatively new initiative at **Halliburton's Energy Services Group**. One of the world's largest providers of oil field services and industrial infrastructure construction and maintenance, Halliburton has operations in more than 100 countries. The company's Energy Services Group, accounting for more than two-thirds of sales, provides well evaluation, construction of production facilities, offshore drilling, and well maintenance services for the oil and gas industry.

Halliburton's Energy Services Group recognizes the traditional definition of knowledge management: get the right information to the right people at the right time. This succinct definition has been helpful in getting Halliburton's employees to understand knowledge management and move forward with profitable and rewarding projects.

The beginning—In 2001 the CEO launched a KM core group in order to become a real-time knowledge company servicing the upstream petroleum industry. The team had 45 days to develop a framework and road map whereby improved knowledge sharing could favorably impact the cost of poor quality, a strategic business objective. Through this effort the team identified a way to proceed and designed a project framework. Using this framework as a springboard, three pilot projects were initiated in late 2001.

Halliburton's Energy Services Group has been able to quickly identify what makes KM work well at Halliburton.

- Each business owns its KM solution. The community of practice must be the business' solution to its own problem for it to work.
- The Energy Services Group develops communities and systems that improve the business, such as improving service quality and customer satisfaction. There must be a valid business case to move forward.
- Community development focuses on building human relationships. The real power in KM is making the connection among people, not deploying IT tools.
- Full-time knowledge brokers facilitate community activity. People who are not focused on an effort full time can be easily distracted with other tasks and assignments. Communities of practice and the knowledge that each drives into day-to-day operations are tactically and strategically important and must have the focus of full-time employees in the knowledge broker position.
- Having the full-time commitment of a development team helped from building communities of practice with an emphasis on human interaction and focused effort. This approach has kept the primary focus on the people, rather than the supporting technology.
- Each of the projects initiated to date has been successful because the KM core group has provided hands-on facilitation in developing, deploying, and sustaining these communities of practice. This has allowed each development team to quickly face challenges and roadblocks to building a strong community.
- To effectively support multiple communities of practice, it is important to have common IT tools from a support perspective so that knowledge brokers and community of practice members can share across the organization.
- It measures results, monitors, and takes action. Any number that is quoted as a savings or a gain must hit the bottom line, because that is where the shareholders see it. They never see any return on their investment if it is only a soft dollar savings.

The Energy Services Group's initial and long-term efforts for knowledge management focused on supporting the overarching objectives of the business. Each potential project is weighed against the Energy Services Group's objectives:

- reduce the cost of poor quality by improving productivity, increasing efficiency, reducing operation costs, and standardizing best practices;
- improve quality of products and services and reduce errors, rework, and cycle time;
- improve customer service;
- build a knowledge-sharing culture; and
- innovate to produce new products and services.

KM activities—The Energy Services Group's basic knowledge management framework is focused on providing the end user with knowledge and information to meet customer needs. As currently fielded, end users search through the knowledge management repositories. If that information is not available, then the end user will work with a knowledge broker, who acts as a human information clearing house for information by linking those who have a need with those who have the information. The knowledge broker will find the information using the subject matter experts and other tools available to him or her. Once the information has been found, the knowledge broker then updates the repository, and the end user puts the identified solution into action to satisfy the customer's needs.

The foundation of the knowledge management system is a strong KM core group, which facilitates developing, launching, and sustaining knowledge management solutions that support each business line's objectives. The KM core group provides a number of services in support of a matrix-structured organization where people report to multiple supervisors and functions. Although the KM core group reports through the R&D technology organization, it works directly with all functions and organizations in the Energy Services Group.

The Energy Services Group's current knowledge management initiatives are focused on two established activities: communities of practice and content management. Developing communities of practice for business improvement or discipline focus that help decrease the cost of poor quality is the primary focus of knowledge management effort for the Energy Services Group. These communities of practice are developed by using small development teams facilitated by the KM core group and applying a rigorous project methodology that has an emphasis on human relations rather than IT utilities. Once deployed, a full-time knowledge broker facilitates continued community sharing. Business improvement communities are developed and deployed in four months, and single-discipline communities are developed in two months.

Although the majority of the effort is focused on communities of practice, content management—in its early stages of use—is developed and deployed on a project-by-project basis where value can be achieved. Plans were in the works to roll out a significant program late in 2003 to improve content management at the individual end user level.

The business case—Knowledge management was driven from the beginning by then-CEO of the Energy Services Group. The original business case developed by the KM core group provided expectations for knowledge management pilot projects that the benefits obtained were expected to be at least twice the cost of implementation. No monetary value was allocated to the less tangible benefits such as enhanced innovation, morale improvements, and improved knowledge retention. The primary objective of the pilots was to improve service quality, but customer satisfaction improvements were also anticipated. The long-term benefit was designed to be an organizational transformation that would make knowledge sharing a natural part of work.

The business case for most projects has been to reduce the cost of poor quality that is systematically tracked in the Energy Services Group. Each potential knowledge management initiative is evaluated and selected based on the strength of its business case and the potential for achieving a satisfactory ROI.

There are two key arguments that have been useful in gaining support for knowledge management activities. The most compelling argument for moving forward with any project has been a good potential ROI. Through the initial work performed in 2001 and early

2002 by the KM core group, the Energy Services Group found that 30 percent to 40 percent of the time, the knowledge or information does not flow to the people who need it while performing their job duties and because of that, problems occur. The second key argument in support of this effort is that management has personally seen the support for knowledge management at a grassroots level through involvement in the communities of practice. As an unplanned benefit, the Energy Services Group has seen an unexpected improvement in the morale of the people who participate in the communities of practice.

The biggest barrier in developing the business case for projects has been the use of knowledge management terminology and language, which served as a roadblock to communication within the organization. The KM core group is very conscious of this and communicates using the natural language of Halliburton.

Whereas the Energy Services Group has been able to consistently develop and deploy thriving and successful communities of practice, it is expected by company leaders in knowledge management that future implementations will have to deliver faster time-to-market, speed in innovation, and productivity increases.

Funding—Knowledge management is funded through the R&D budget. The first year knowledge management core costs appeared in the form of a non-itemized indirect allocation to the various business units/departments. In 2003 knowledge management core costs appeared as an indirect itemized allocation to each business unit/ department so that business units can see what they are paying for. The knowledge broker and global knowledge champion are funded by the organization that receives the benefit of the community.

Measuring KM—The Energy Services Group's basic philosophy surrounding measurement is best described as: no measurements, no results. In Halliburton, if you are not measuring something, then you are not doing anything.

Knowledge management measurements are defined and agreed on by the community sponsors and process owners early in the development of communities of practice. Before moving past the design phase, a meeting is held between the design team and the stakeholders to review the measures and gain agreement that they are the correct measures to evaluate the activity's impact on business objectives.

The Energy Services Group identifies input and process measures that track portal activity within the communities. These metrics are automatically collected and reported in real time for users. Output and outcome measures that track the actual transfer of knowledge and its impact on operations are measured using traditional business measures that indicate the impact on business objectives, such as efficiency, reduction in cost of poor quality, and time to repair. Some of the differences between what are considered process measures and impact, or output and outcome, measures follow.

Process measures include portal usage metrics, which are automatically collected and displayed, and collaboration activity that relates to community activity. Impact measures include: end-of-job customers dissatisfaction (Halliburton Management System), the average time to repair (SAP), duplicate work orders (SAP), maintenance cost reductions (SAP), jobs not invoices (SAP), stories from the knowledge management community, and lost hours from top ten causes of failure.

Results and the bottom line—The Energy Services Group invested $3.2 million USD to develop, launch, and sustain the KM initiative and its activities in 2002, with $2.6 million USD being allocated to the core KM initiative. The investment was split along these lines: 70 percent for personnel, 20 percent for IT-related costs, and 10 percent for other. The Energy Services Group calculates that it achieved in excess of $4.8 million USD in bottom-line benefits in 2002, a first year ROI of 50 percent.

For an organization that had its first serious conversations surrounding knowledge management in 2001, the Energy Services Group has achieved so much. Some of the more significant achievements in the initial 18 months are:

- 23 percent improvement in average time to repair;
- 53 percent improvement in electronic technician user satisfaction survey;
- 50 percent reduction in end-of-job customer dissatisfaction;
- 78 percent improvement in perforating failures attributed to the top ten causes;

- knowledge management communities now have 17,000 collaboration hits with 3,100 unique users per month, 489 issues raised, and 386 issues resolved per month, in an average of 3.8 days; and
- documented 50 percent ROI created in 2002.

One community, focused on production enhancement, saw maintenance costs decline from $4.5 million to $3 million USD from 2001 to 2002. All of the eight communities that started in the first year will continue with minimal additional investment, beyond the time of the participants. The value added during 2002 provided Halliburton's knowledge management group with solid evidence of the program's success. The organization's investment in its KM initiative for 2002 was $3.2 million. Its value added that year was $4.8 million, which meant the ROI was $1.6 million, or 50 percent. Based on their initial success, other communities are in the process of launching.

Among the leaders in almost every market in which it competes, **IBM** makes desktop and notebook PCs, mainframes and servers, storage systems, and peripherals and also has a growing services business.

The beginning—IBM has been active in knowledge management since the 1980s. Over the years, as IBM brought disparate business units together, data management evolved to information management and then to knowledge management. However, the real trigger for knowledge management within IBM came in the 1990s when the company reorganized under new leadership with the concept of providing a seamless experience to its customers. Leadership believed that knowledge management was the means for achieving that end. Knowledge management efforts in IBM span three areas: internal knowledge management offerings and services, external offerings and services, and research. The internal focus began in 1994 within the services business. As IBM moved into services as part of its overall strategy and shifted to providing solutions rather than technology to its customers, it realized a need to share knowledge across its business and within its businesses better than it had been doing in the past.

In 1998 a corporate knowledge management effort, KMBlue, was established to raise awareness of knowledge management among all the business units. In 2001 the corporate knowledge management mission was brought under the Office of the Business Transformation and CIO (BT/CIO). At that time, the mission broadened to include setting the overall knowledge management direction for IBM, providing knowledge management leadership, and deploying corporate knowledge management infrastructure and solutions.

KM activities—IBM's knowledge management approach and strategy focuses on four elements whose integration are key to creating and sustaining a knowledge-based business: expertise, content, collaboration, and learning. In addition, it focuses on how these elements are leveraged by different social systems (that is, how knowledge is shared by individuals as well as members of teams and communities).

Expertise involves the ability to find and work with subject matter experts across the business and then leverage their knowledge and experience. Content management is the ability to access pertinent information immediately and easily. Collaboration refers to the ability for two (or more) people to work together through time and space. Learning, or e-learning, is the ability to receive just-in-time mentoring and education to develop a career and job-related skill set.

The objectives for knowledge management efforts across the organization vary depending on business need. The goal may be improved efficiency, competency, responsiveness, or innovation.

IBM's KM core group and leaders support knowledge management activities across the business units by ensuring that the strategy, vision, and value systems support current and future activities. Once this underlying structure is in place and aligned with the business objectives, the core team of knowledge management leaders provides support to address the management system. This takes the form of establishing roles, responsibilities, and processes and providing technology support. Additionally, the core group ensures that the incentives and measurements of the business are aligned.

The KM core group and leaders discourage programs that focus solely on technology. Instead, they encourage any program to have both a technology and business transformation component to it.

Knowledge management activities at IBM span a wide range. However, three key activities currently receiving a lot of attention and focus are expertise locator systems, communities of practice, and the facilitated transfer of best practices.

Although IBM has had databases containing people information in various business units for several years, the corporation actively began focusing on expertise locator systems in 2001. This is a shift in focus from collection to connection. IBM's executives understand that connecting people to people and, therefore, to expertise, is critical to the business. IBM already had a corporate directory that provided name, number, secretary, organizational structure, e-mail address, and more. In 2001 it extended its corporate directory with what it calls "Persona," which elaborates on a person's profile. The objective is to have the involvement of all the business units in this corporate solution.

Expert locator systems are a key initiative for the KM core group, and a large challenge for them as well. Not only are they trying to connect people on a global scale, but they also must deal with turnover, which for an organization of 300,000 plus people, can be significant. Additionally, there are acquisitions, such as PwC Consulting, to deal with. Making people aware of the skills possessed by their colleagues, even those working thousands of miles away, is a tremendous concern for the KM core group and IBM.

Communities of practice have existed at IBM for many years and have been formally recognized since 1995. They have evolved extensively over the years, and some are fairly sophisticated. Much of the evolution communities have experienced occurred in the process of managing and supporting them. Originally, there was an overall group that helped support communities; but as the communities matured, that support has been pushed further into the line of business so that they are now supported at the business level. The global services unit is a primary focus for communities of practice because it aligns well with the business model. There are about 75 active communities in global services, and they receive varying degrees of focus, attention, and support.

One example of facilitated best practices transfer is in the project management community, which has approximately 4,400 members.

It also has a Center of Excellence that encourages the 18,000 IBM project managers to exchange lessons they have learned on projects and project management tools.

A second example is in the global services function. In global services, the focus is on community exchange because the communities in this area were designed to implement knowledge transfer. Global services also has a tremendous amount of content it manages from client engagements. Because the content is used to increase the efficiency of solution delivery to clients, the management process is rigorous and conducted by subject matter experts within each community.

The business case—Knowledge management was formally recognized in IBM in 1995 and at the time was technology-driven. With the formation of global services in 1996, IBM's KM initiative began to come together. When IBM developed global services, it made sure that knowledge management was built into the infrastructure of the business. Prior to that time, IBM did not possess a knowledge management methodology, processes, or systems necessary to run a services business, so it was built from scratch. The business case was crucial and, at the same time, easy to make because the company had increased the staff size to run a services organization.

The addition of the global services infrastructure compelled IBM to develop a KM initiative because the company needed to know what it knew. According to the site visit representative, a services business cannot be run without knowledge management because the product is knowledge. Some of IBM's product divisions have had less success with knowledge management efforts because they focus on a product instead of knowledge. It may be that the need for knowledge is more readily apparent in the service business.

In 2003 the executives of IBM viewed knowledge management as the cost of doing business. Company representatives stated that the company was at a point of sustaining knowledge management. The business continues to invest in it in much the same way it does its finance or HR systems. However, with an annual funding model such as the one used by IBM, it is necessary to regularly update stakeholders and manage their expectations. Budgets can be cut, so it is important to keep this group up-to-date and aware of what is happening with relevant knowledge management activities and programs. That means measures must be collected and reported regularly. IBM has a monthly corporate reporting cycle that helps manage these expectations.

The business case for knowledge management evolves as the imperatives of the business change. IBM is evolving to the next generation of e-business, what it calls e-business "on demand." This will require some changes to the KM initiatives as the business strategy changes. As IBM's business strategy starts to evolve, the KM initiatives required to support that strategy need to adapt and evolve as well. Those that do so successfully will continue to receive funding.

Funding—IBM uses an annual funding model with project reviews at standard checkpoints. This model includes a formal process for requests to receive funding. Knowledge management is no exception. The process involves investment review boards and funding boards, and a program must be reviewed by each board to receive funding for a given year. Additionally, reviews are held at critical checkpoints to ensure programs are on track and still have executive sponsorship and stakeholder support. IBM executes this funding model at all levels of the business, and reallocation of funding requires a new business case.

Measuring KM—IBM does not measure knowledge management per se. Instead, it measures the business results achieved when it implements a knowledge management initiative in that business. The eight steps that follow determine the value of KM initiatives.

1. Determine business objectives and strategy and how the knowledge management initiative will help to achieve those goals.
2. Determine the purpose of the knowledge management solutions to be implemented.
3. Determine who will use measures and how they will be used.
4. Determine which measurement framework is best.
5. Determine what should be measured.
6. Determine how the measures will be collected and analyzed.
7. Determine what can be learned from the measures and what actions should be taken.
8. Revisit the business objectives and align measurements.

The KM core group is responsible for measurement. Group members identify output measures or results and the process measures that are relevant to the results. They also identify the practices that indicate what goals are being attained and how. For example, in expertise location, they know how many people have Persona pages. However, just knowing that number does not tell them the value people receive from that information. It does tell them the level of participation, though. Therefore, they know what kind of penetration they are getting with the tool and how relevant it is across the business.

For IBM's expertise locator system, Persona, the KM core group uses a Web-based survey to determine user satisfaction with the tool. The annual survey allows for write-in comments, which are analyzed by the group to determine main points. In addition to the survey data, the core group also analyzes the total number of Persona pages created compared to when the last measurement was taken. The group looks at traffic on the pages on a weekly basis and measures the number of page views, searches, updates, and unique visitors. The core group also looks at this data on a country-by-country basis to understand trends in use and where there might be problems, perhaps due to language barriers. This information is immediately distributed to all members of the BT/CIO community and to IBM employees at a later date via a Web article.

IBM estimates the savings from the use of Persona pages by enabling people to find the right resources more quickly.

At IBM, collaboration tools link closely with expertise tools. IBM's wide range of collaboration tools provides solutions across the board, from same time/same place to any time/any place. Their use, however, depends on the culture of the business. To determine employee satisfaction with its collaboration tools, IBM uses a Web-based customer satisfaction survey. Again, the results of the survey are distributed immediately to all members of the BT/CIO community and later to all IBM employees via a Web article.

Web conferences enable IBM employees to conduct effective virtual meetings. To determine the degree of participation in the Web conferencing program, the process owner looks at monthly participation levels, the number of Web conferences hosted weekly and monthly, and the average length of time a conference is held. These figures are available each month online for a set group of individuals to use in reporting forward. IBM estimates savings of approximately $50 million USD in cost avoidance through the use of Web conferencing.

It may sound simplistic, but many times a measure is picked because it can be measured. That is, the KM core group knows the data already exists or that it can get the data to support the measure. Data availability is crucial in the measurement process. Another issue is whether information can be collected without overburdening people.

Some measurements are good for the KM initiatives, and some measurements are good for the business. For example, data on how much IBM saves using Web conferencing resonates with executives. One crucial step is to identify the five most useful measures for both the KM initiatives and the business and act on those.

The metrics easiest to obtain are those that can be derived directly from an application because they do not require much time from people in the business units. These measures are designed into an application as part of the development plan. Other measures are obtained via a survey. However, because surveys proliferated, the company actually had to put an employee survey registry process in place to approve all surveys directed at more than 100 people. The problem is under better control now with certain large surveys administered annually.

Additionally, some communities administer smaller surveys, or polls, among their members to get feedback. The surveys yield not only data, but also content that helps the KM core group understand future directions.

Results—At the corporate level, IBM's KM core group focuses on tangible deliverables. They do recognize the value in intangible deliverables, but these are harder to measure. The key is to ensure the executives understand what the core program really provides. Otherwise, resources may be cut, which would result in inefficiencies. Fortunately, there are some great successes.

First, Web conferencing provides a virtual space for collaboration with other employees or customers, with an average of 33,000 worldwide participants per month joining more than 6,000 internal and outbound Web conferences. Savings are estimated at $50 million USD per year in travel costs (time and expense) avoidance minimum. Forums are topic-based discussion vehicles and/or repositories and are frequently the primary method of communication for online communities. Questions are posed by participants and answered by forum authors (peers and interested parties) on a volunteer basis. Nearly 17,000 authors participated in at least one of more than 1,000 forums in December 2002. Web forums result in an estimated cost avoidance of $6 million USD annually because participants find information more quickly and avoid rework.

Employee-created Persona pages facilitate the identification and location of subject matter experts based on an individual's projects, teams, expertise, and business interests. There are currently 111,000 Persona pages. The estimated savings from finding the right resources more quickly are $5.5 million USD annually.

Finally, the "CommunityMap" enables individual IBM employees to locate communities and communities to locate individual employees. People can browse a taxonomy of topics associated with communities to find entries for each community. Within each entry, they can read enough information to decide whether they want to join the community, as well as find instructions for joining. Community leaders can also create entries on the map so that IBM employees can find them. There are 82 registered communities, and the map receives 2,400 hits per month.

Feedback from senior management concerning the impact on business confirmed the positive impact knowledge management was having on the organization and the benefits it was receiving as a result of the investment.

The final example, which may be more relevant to readers from the nonprofit and government sectors, does not have a traditional bottom-line measure of success, but rather numerable indicators of how it has successfully benefited from becoming a learning organization.

The World Bank helps the poorest people in the poorest countries by maximizing opportunities and cushioning the shocks to those countries as they become involved in the world economy. With 10,000 professionals in 109 countries, the World Bank states that it is not a bank in the common sense. It is one of the United Nations' specialized agencies and is made up of 184 member countries. As of 2003, the World Bank was involved in more than 1,800 projects in virtually every sector and developing country.

The World Bank also plays a vital role in coordinating with other organizations—private, government, multilateral, and nongovernment—to ensure that resources are used to their full effect in supporting a country's developmental agenda. Without the exchange of knowledge, everyone will make the same mistakes or inevitably have to reinvent the wheel. A central core of knowledge is needed that draws on the experience of the World Bank and the people in the field. This central core of knowledge is called the knowledge bank.

The beginning—Because the World Bank has been providing lending and advisory services throughout the world for 50 years, it has become a repository of experience and best practices. In 1996 the president of the World Bank, James D. Wolfensohn, announced that knowledge management would be a key strategy for the organization as it deals with problems in the future. This announcement meant a profound change in the way the World Bank conducted its business. Wolfensohn's vision encompassed the dissemination of the World Bank's knowledge to external clients and partners, not merely to internal staff.

The strategy progressively evolved through learning by doing. Large numbers of staff members were involved in creating the implementation plan, extrapolating the experience it had already acquired, and learning from other organizations by participating in benchmarking exercises with APQC. Upper management support led to greater resources for KM efforts and great experimentation and risk taking.

The overall idea for knowledge sharing came from the top, but the ideas concerning how to implement the strategy came from the bottom. To implement the strategy, the World Bank focused on several initiatives. These initiatives were coordinated by the small, central knowledge-sharing unit, initially through a formal knowledge management board, but later through a less formal knowledge-sharing community. The World Bank realized that the most critical knowledge to capture is the context in which the actions occurred. What became important was for a group or person with information to tell a story to a subject matter expert, who could ask probing questions to guide the conversation beyond the action steps taken to the overall decision-making process.

As of 1997, KM activities began to include:

- regular staff meetings,
- knowledge management open houses where information was presented to several hundred people,
- a knowledge fair that reached several thousand people in the organization,
- an online presence,
- brochures and pamphlets on knowledge management, and
- *The World Development Report* on knowledge for development aimed at putting knowledge on the world agenda.

The business case—Reasons for sharing knowledge included a large cadre of staff retiring due to natural attrition and early retirement plans. Also, staff returning from working the field offices or having completed assignments had acquired vast amounts of knowledge regarding local social and political conditions. Neither group had a medium to share its wealth of information with others.

At the World Bank, speed, quality, innovation, and wider external access to know-how were also powerful drivers. What convinced the World Bank of its need for knowledge management was its belief that it could not succeed, even in its existing lending business, unless it could present the best global know-how to its clients. Knowledge sharing became an internal business necessity. Plus, the World Bank realized it could not succeed in its mission of poverty reduction unless it used its knowledge in new ways to reach partners, stakeholders, and civil society.

To convince the organization to buy into this strategy of knowledge as a business necessity, the World Bank leaders demonstrated the value of knowledge management in two ways. First, they pointed out the business value of internal knowledge by explaining that, even in lending, the World Bank's clients would no longer be interested in its advice unless it could mobilize the relevant global experience and use it to address each client's specific problems.

The second argument used by the World Bank leaders dealt with the business value of external knowledge sharing. Knowledge sharing emerged as a business necessity because the World Bank realized that lending alone could not possibly accomplish poverty reduction.

KM activities—At the World Bank, knowledge management was designed to systematically capture and organize the wealth of knowledge and experience gained from staff, clientele, and development partners; make this knowledge readily accessible to a wide audience internally and externally; and create links between groups and communalities working on similar topics. Knowledge sharing at the World Bank would focus on:

- putting knowledge on par with money,
- learning from clients and partners,
- reinforcing continuous learning,
- building client capacity and widening partnerships, and
- promoting an open environment for effective knowledge sharing.

In 2002, after six years of developing a knowledge-sharing strategy, the World Bank felt it had firmly established its three pillars of knowledge sharing.

1. **Sharing knowledge within the World Bank**—mentoring and coaching programs, orientation, debriefings, communities of practice (thematic groups), and advisory services
2. **Sharing knowledge and working with clients**—networks, indigenous knowledge, and the development forum
3. **Enhancing the capacity of clients**—learning and innovation loans, global knowledge initiatives, and its consultative group on international agricultural research.

The initial main elements of the knowledge management system for the World Bank were as follows.

- **Managing knowledge**—Managing knowledge involves generating new knowledge through both formal research and learning via the networks; capturing information and knowledge through the systematic assembling of existing information; project debriefing on each major milestone; commissioning contributions by World Bank experts in subject areas; pulling, reviewing, and analyzing information from existing internal and external sources; and drawing on discussions from electronic discussion tools and online communities. Distribution mechanisms would include both help desks and electronic systems.

- **Cutting-edge knowledge**—Unless cutting-edge knowledge is created through learning, formal research, and knowledge from outside the organization, organizing and disseminating knowledge will be of little value. Hence, the foundation of managing knowledge is the knowledge-creation process.

- **Processes for organizing knowledge**—Processes are being put into place to ensure the quality of the material in the system, to ensure that appropriate classification procedures are established and followed to enable fast retrieval, and to enable appropriate access for potential internal and external users. Material would be organized and categorized within the overall framework of the World Bank-wide architecture, which reflected the viewpoints that system users would need, including geography, sector, and process. The system would require substantial efforts to maintain the quality of knowledge content through developing new material as new issues and findings emerge, updating the existing material and architecture, and weeding out material that has become obsolete. The entire system would comprise both divergent processes to incorporate new information and insights and convergent processes to synthesize and distill information into key findings. Feedback mechanisms would be put in place to help the knowledge management system evolve to meet changing user requirements, through both helpdesks and user surveys.

- **A demand-driven system**—The content of the system depends on user interest and demand. Likely components would include helpdesks to answer queries and provide resource maps and information packets; databases including terms of reference, consultants, lessons learned, key articles and books, papers, reports, and what's new; and knowledgeable bases including sector strategies, tool kits, model outputs, analytical tools, best practices, and sources of information.

- **Quality control**—The knowledge management system would aim to improve quality control on the ground through being demand-driven, accessible, timely, authoritative, efficient, inclusive, user-friendly, sustainable, consistent, scalable, flexible, and iterative. The system would aspire to achieve the highest level of quality and would be periodically benchmarked against knowledge management systems of organizations considered to be the leaders in the field.

- **Culture shift**—The more difficult aspect of the knowledge bank would be the necessary organizational culture shift away from an individualistic mode of working and storing knowledge toward a sharing team mode of work. Measures would include: a) facilitation of sharing through easier access by World Bank professionals to tools for publishing material within the knowledge management system itself, b) provision of adequate budget for work related to knowledge sharing, c) changes in the personnel evaluation system to recognize and encourage knowledge sharing, and d) other formal and informal measures needed to change the culture. A sustained leadership effort was undertaken for the culture shift to succeed.

- **Training and communications**—Even though technology is a key enabler, knowledge management is fundamentally about people, not machines. The objective would be to create true knowledge managers, not merely to proliferate databases containing large quantities of low-quality information that creates more work rather than saves time. Helpdesks and formal training would need to be supplemented by workshops, seminars, brown-bag lunches, and informal personal gatherings (including mentoring) that provide much of the learning, sharing, and intellectual growth among colleagues. In the end, people are the key determinant of success.

- **Knowledge classification scheme**—A common classification scheme for knowledge across all networks and units is a key driver of the effectiveness of technology used in a knowledge management system. The World Bank must focus on a common set of design rules and practices that are valid for all operational units. With the use of object-oriented technology, the schemes can be readily extended to cover the specialized requirements of a knowledge management system. The aim is to develop a technology solution that is flexible enough to accommodate a variety of needs, yet has a common organization scheme. This would allow for efficient sharing of information, even if the inputs should come from different areas. This would be consistently classified and searchable.

In the process of implementing its knowledge management strategy, the World Bank learned that neither connecting nor collecting could be effectively achieved unless communities of practice where in place. The World Bank noted in 2000 that the nurturing of such communities (known in the World Bank as thematic groups) had become a central preoccupation of the knowledge management program. To facilitate the exchange of knowledge, the World Bank changed its working structure from a geographic organization structure to a matrix organization structure. Within the matrix, teams of people with the same skills and responsibilities, regardless of location, formed thematic groups. They are organized by sector or across sector and support core World Bank functions. By 2000, more than 100 thematic groups existed.

These communities can be problem focused, cross disciplinary, work process focused, or product focused; basically they are organized any way you can think of to get a group of people together to tackle a problem. Some of the activities the thematic groups are responsible for include building the knowledge base and the quality of knowledge and reaching out to new members. Given the size and scope of the World Bank, the organization must consider all angles of a problem at nearly the same time. Consequently, its communities of practice do not fit a neat description. The organization is also developing communities outside its organization to involve all stakeholders and create a network of communities.

Other activities include the World Bank's corporate knowledge and learning organization, known as the World Bank Institute, which assists in transferring skills and knowledge sharing for both client and staff development. It focuses on trans-thematic areas by integrating knowledge from different thematic groups.

Funding—The World Bank has invested $50 million USD per year on the total knowledge-sharing program; most of these funds are used to allocate two staff weeks per optional staff member per year to the knowledge program. This focus and allocation of resources has helped the World Bank develop ideas and obtain results. A knowledge manager in each organizational or business unit is responsible for both the budget and implementation of knowledge-sharing activities in that unit. Overall coordination of all knowledge-sharing activities is accomplished by a four-person, central knowledge-sharing unit. The coordinating unit builds communities across KM support activities, including knowledge manager, advisory services, and CoP levels.

Measuring KM and results—The World Bank has monitored and evaluated the effectiveness of its KM processes almost from the start in 1996. Inputs, activities, outputs, and even outcomes have been measured.

The World Bank measures the inputs into KM, such as how much is being spent and the number of programs. It also measures the outputs, which involve the number of best practices, new tools, knowledge nuggets, resources added, or processes put in place. The third aspect of measurement is the use of knowledge products and services, such as the number of unique visitors to a Web site, the number of queries on an information and statistics system, or the number of requests for services from advisory services. The World Bank also conducts internal client surveys. Each of the sector boards surveys the community concerning the most effective knowledge products and how frequently they are used, as well as the respondent's contribution in the last year.

The World Bank also uses a staff survey for the entire organization, which asks a range of questions, including some focused on KM. These questions focus on "the extent to which people feel they have access to knowledge to do their work" and "the extent to which global knowledge is perceived to be available to clients." Additionally, a number of external surveys have been conducted in the African region by asking main counterparts in government project offices about improvement in access to the World Bank's knowledge and how well the World Bank adapts global knowledge to local conditions. In 2003 it was reported that people responded positively to the first but less so to the second, which indicated that the World Bank still has room to improve in knowledge adaptation.

The World Bank uses a variety of methods to acquire feedback from end users of its KM support technology, including focus groups; surveys both on paper and online; groupware used in conducting focus groups; comments solicited, collected, and responded to through feedback channels as part of online development; and organization-wide feedback gathered as part of the staff survey.

Feedback in focus groups has usually been solicited with a particular purpose in mind, and the inputs have been used in the decision making. More generic feedback mechanisms, such as the staff survey, have a process to address the most important issues. The feedback on knowledge was among the more positive results of the survey, so it did not figure into the action planning. And there was no need for a specific follow-up.

The World Bank believes the effectiveness of its improvement efforts is best judged by participants. Inside the organization, employees are conscious of what remains to be done. In particular, the culture shift is well on its way, but it still has some way to go.

CHAPTER 6

Moving Forward

In our minds, this is all about creating capacity in the organization to get these business goals, which we could not hit without some kind of new way of thinking about what the organization knew, what the organization needed to know, what we needed to learn, and then how we wanted to move ahead. We started to look for some small wins that could leverage a little bit of capacity that we could then leverage against the bigger opportunities.

— Todd K. Abraham, vice president of strategic technology and knowledge management, the Pillsbury Company, speaking at APQC's conference *Knowledge Management: Lessons from the Leading Edge.*

You may be asking yourself, "Where do I go from here?" As I advised in my book *If Only We Knew What We Know: The Transfer of Internal Knowledge and Best Practice*, there are a number of initial steps to take. Let's look at how to proceed.

Step 1   Get smart. Understand knowledge-sharing behaviors and support systems. Read. Benchmark. Get feedback.

Step 2   Start planning. Assess just where you stand on the KM learning curve. Identify your business strategy component in need of support. You need to know where you are now and where to go before you embark on any change efforts.

Step 3   Set the guiding principles, and define the need. Your involvement in this step will mitigate resistance and change management questions. Executive involvement and periodic meetings ensure you know any risks or issues that come up and react accordingly. The "right" knowledge management approach depends on the context and the need.

Step 4   Find the processes and projects that support your value proposition, inform the rest of the organization, and demand a solid business case.

Step 5   Select pilot projects that give your organization a good chance of early success and a testing ground for technologies and methods.

Step 6   Follow tried-and-true principles of design, such as employing a multidisciplinary KM core group and sound change management principals. Get buy-in and understanding in the organization.

Step 7   Guide the implementation and launch of your projects. Ensure employees are properly trained and results and lessons are accurately documented.

Step 8   Apply what you have learned from the pilots in an expansion strategy that embeds KM into every area of the organization.

Step 9   Sustain your improvements, and plan to scale up.

Throughout the book, I have provided a number of principles to guide you through implementing and sustaining a successful KM initiative. Here are some parting tips to get the most impact from knowledge management.

- The measurement of knowledge management is only meaningful if you understand what drives your value proposition.

- Develop a long-term vision with short- and mid-term measures. Focus on the long-term outcomes of your immediate actions.

- Connect people to people. People do not know what they know until they are asked.

- Communities of practice are a powerful and unique enabler of knowledge flow and creation. Explore where CoPs would help.

- Be prepared to invest in not only technology, but also knowledge capture, content management, developing taxonomies, and educating employees.

- Look for teachable moments, and put information where people will trip over it.

- If you simply build it, they will not come. Providing access to knowledge is not the end step. Facilitate the heck out of this, and engage the targeted knowledge recipients.

- Supply magnet content. To be successful, best practices and knowledge transfer must help people do their jobs better and faster, be embedded in the work itself, and be self-reinforcing and self-generating. Focus on the users' needs: How will this help improve their day?

- Make it ridiculously easy for people to share. Embed knowledge flows in the work flow. Good technology really does matter.
- Recognize and measure the appropriate actions and achievements.
- Measure the value, not just the activity.
- Watch how your culture changes as a result of knowledge sharing.

As you move forward, keep in mind that progress will sometimes be frustrating, erratic, and challenging. Some people just will not seem to "get it." But success will come from viewing knowledge management as a central principle to your organization remaining competitive.

A knowledge management initiative, if successful, never ends. Many organizations have made significant gains through their knowledge management initiatives, but the true leaders of each industry will make efforts to sustain those gains by measuring and monitoring knowledge management activities. New technologies, customer demands, shifting work forces, and regulatory issues will require the structure of the knowledge management initiative to be revisited. And an executive may need to strongly reinforce knowledge management principles in times of mergers, work force issues, and marketplace challenges by providing continuity in knowledge-sharing policies and leadership by example.

Thomas Davenport once said, "Knowledge managers may feel that if they could only get their organization's knowledge under control, their work would be done. However, the tasks of knowledge management are never-ending."

A successful KM initiative will be integrated into all business approaches, as employees examine all processes for knowledge flows. Executives must keep a number of questions at the forefront of their work forces: What information can be used later? What is needed to be more effective? Who has that information, and who needs it? The question to then ask yourself is: How can I bring those people together?

As is regularly demanded of executives, I advise that you be prepared to quickly adjust and expand your knowledge management activities as required to meet customer demands. There is no ideal in knowledge management, and there are always more opportunities to exact gains from your knowledge management efforts.

Knowledge Management

Glossary of Terms

- **Absorptive capacity**—The ability of a group to recognize the value of new, external information, assimilate it, and apply it to commercial ends. It is largely a function of the group's level of prior related knowledge, which could include: basic skills, shared language, knowledge of recent scientific or industry developments, technology, and culture.

- **Acquired knowledge**—A source of knowledge from outside of the organization. The knowledge can be purchased or "rented."

- **Active participation**—Active participation can include being a member in communities, being a content manager, using the expertise locator system, and sharing best practices. Using a corporate portal per se is not considered participation.

- **Adaptation**—Knowledge that results from responding to new processes or technologies in the market place. If organizations do not adapt, they will cease to remain competitive.

- **Advisory board**—A cross-functional advisory team that represents respected thought leaders throughout the organization, typically made up of vice president and director-level people. The purpose of the advisory board is to:
  - provide a forum for surfacing, addressing, and solving shared knowledge management issues and needs;
  - create, capture, and leverage knowledge management best practices and approaches;
  - support communities of practice and collaboration methods for transfer of high-value tacit knowledge;
  - communicate knowledge management messages and successes (internally and externally); and
  - advocate and support common processes for knowledge access, management, and use.

- **Aggregator**—An organization that combines information such as news, sports scores, weather forecasts, and reference materials from various sources and makes it available to its customers (source: *TechWeb Technology Encyclopedia*).

- **After-Action Reviews**—Pioneered by the U.S. Army, structured After-Action Review meetings capture key lessons from participants at significant project milestones or upon completion of a project or important action. Typically the questions addressed include "What was supposed to happen?", "What actually happened?", and "What would we do differently in the future?" The lessons are captured so that other teams can plan and act more effectively to avoid repeating mistakes.

- **Assessment tools**—A listing of guidelines for using criteria to evaluate a given situation. The guidelines might be a scoring or priority system.

- **Best practices**—An assessment recommending the most appropriate way of handling a certain type of task, based on an observation of the way that several organizations handle that task.

- **Communities of practice**—Designated networks of people that share information and knowledge. Community members share, collaborate, and learn from one another face-to-face and virtually. Communities are held together by a common goal and desire to share experiences, insights, and best practices within a topic or discipline using shared norms and processes. Communities also may be accountable for capturing best practices and stewarding a body of knowledge on behalf of the organization. Communities may be formally launched and have community leaders, stewards, or gatekeepers. This approach may be supported by collaborative technologies and content management systems to convert tacit knowledge that emerges through dialogue or response to questions into explicit knowledge that can be categorized and stored for future reuse and reference.

- **Content management system**—A system to provide meaningful and timely information to end users by creating processes that identify, collect, categorize, and refresh content using a common taxonomy across the organization. A content management system includes people, processes, technology, and most importantly, the content itself. Content is broadly defined as all the explicit artifacts produced by work, such as documents, databases, presentations, and e-mail—virtually any artifact of transactions, dialogue, or creative work that is inside or outside the organization. Content may also include external content (news feeds, subscriptions to data and analysis, and publications) and content from the extended enterprise (suppliers, customers, vendors, consultants, and external sales).

- **Core group**—The staff who provides central leadership in coordination of the knowledge management initiative, IT applications designed to support knowledge management and collaboration, and common methodologies. The core group does not include employees in business units who may be leading a community of practice.
- **Data**—Facts and figures presented out of context for the purpose of innovation or improved efficiency.
- **Database**—A collection of related information, which is structured for easy access to specific pieces of information.
- **Data mining**—A process of reviewing information in a database and making new connections among the information.
- **Decision-support system**—A computer application that analyzes business data and presents it so that users can make business decisions more easily. Typical information that a decision-support application might gather and present would be comparative sales figures, project revenue figures based on new product sales, and the consequences of various decision alternatives, given past experience in a context that is described. (Source: *CIO Magazine*)
- **Dedicated resources**—Knowledge that results from an organization's setting aside some staff members or an entire department (usually R&D) to develop new intellectual property.
- **Expertise locator systems**—The purpose of these systems is to identify people with expertise and link them to those with questions or problems or to staff projects requiring that expertise. Such systems may also be referred to as yellow pages, personal Web pages, expert directories, or profiles. The applications supporting these systems sometimes include content analysis of e-mail and documents to automatically identify staff members who may be working on a topic and connect them with others. These applications connect employees by offering a unified, searchable interface that captures employee interests, skills, and accomplishments. Domain champions or content experts are

sometimes designated to answer questions or determine whether answers are a best practice and should be captured for other repositories.

- **Explicit knowledge**—Knowledge that can be written down or expressed verbally.
- **Facilitated best practices transfer process**—This refers to the discipline around the transfer of best practices within an organization. This approach uses structured processes to capture tacit knowledge, convert it to explicit knowledge, transfer it to a recipient, and measure the business impact of the reuse of that knowledge. It may be used in conjunction with other approaches such as communities of practice.
- **Firewall**—Software that "separates" information so it is only available to users within an organization, not to all users of the World Wide Web. In some instances, the software prompts users to enter an identifying name and password to indicate that they have authority to gain access to the network.
- **Full-time equivalent (FTE)**—Refers to the total number of employees who would work as full-time equivalents (40 hours per week). For example, two part-time employees working 20 hours each would equal one FTE. Likewise, a full-time employee who works 20 hours per week in support of this function and 20 hours per week in the service of another department/process would count as 0.5 FTE.
- **Fusion**—Knowledge created by bringing together people with different perspectives to work on the same project.
- **Human capital**—The knowledge-power that comes and goes from an organization each day. This is another way of describing the knowledge that resides in the heads of employees and that has not been shared with others.
- **Index**—A list (as of bibliographical information or citations to a body of literature) arranged usually in alphabetical order of some specified data (as author, subject, or keyword). A list of items (as topics or names) treated in a printed work that gives for each item the page number where it may be found. (source: *Merriam-Webster Dictionary*)
- **Information**—Data that is presented in context so people might make use of it.

- **Innovation**—Any new idea, method, or device developed by an individual, group, or organization. The embodiment, combination, or synthesis of knowledge into new and unique combinations.
- **Intellectual capital**—An effort by organizations to place a financial value on its tacit and explicit knowledge.
- **Interface**—A link, usually between a computer and a user or among computer programs. An interface between a computer and user refers to the elements of the computer and software that the user interacts with: the screens, icons, menus, and dialogues. An interface among computer programs involves using agreed-upon commands and statements that let one computer program exchange information with the other in a way that the first program can integrate the second program.
- **KM core group**—A cross-functional group that represents the business unit or functional area of a knowledge management initiative. Typically, this group includes both management and line representation. The purpose of the group is to:
  - refine the scope of the pilots or initiatives;
  - identify the pilot users and "high-voltage knowledge" to achieve early success;
  - analyze costs and the infrastructure required;
  - recommend communication, training, rewards, and other issues affecting cultural acceptance of a knowledge management approach; and
  - plan projects with staged activities and milestones.
- **Knowledge**—Information in action; information that people make use of, along with the rules and contexts of its use.
- **Knowledge assets**—Intellectual properties that generate a cash flow for the organization. Examples include patents, copyrighted material, and licenses.
- **Knowledge base**—A central database of information about a particular topic or organization. An infobase typically includes information from all parts of an organization.
- **Knowledge management**—Systematic approaches to help information and knowledge flow to the right people at the right time so they can act more efficiently and effectively. Find, understand, share, and use knowledge to create value.

- **Knowledge networking**—Knowledge resulting from people sharing information with one another formally or informally. Knowledge networking often occurs within disciplines (such as programmers communicating with one another) and projects (such as all of the people working on a new software product sharing information with one another).

- **Leadership and process owners**—Those in business and functional units who make funding and participation decisions (e.g., corporate, sales, operations, and research and development).

- **Lessons learned**—A reflection on knowledge that people should take with them from an experience into similar ones. These lessons often reflect on "what we did right," "what we would do differently," and "how we could improve our process and product to be more effective in the future."

- **Mass customization**—A basic product that is available in a variety of forms, each tailored to a different audience (such as new or experienced users) or need (such as training or marketing). The audience perceives that the information was customized just for them, but the developers of that information do not have to write separate versions of the information for each audience.

- **Meta-tagging**—Classification data that is stored on the computer with the information. Users facilitate the retrieval of it by using agreed-upon terminology as well as formats that software can easily scan.

- **Metcalf's Law**—"Power is a function of the square of the size of the network."

- **Moore's Law**—The phenomenon that the capacity of the microprocessors that form the nucleus of a computer doubles approximately every 18 months. Similar improvements to telecommunications capacity occur approximately every five months.

- **Noncompetitors**—Organizations that do not seek the same business or clients that you do but from whom you might glean best practices and lessons learned. Although neither the best practices nor lessons learned might appear to be relevant at first glance, they can be shown to transfer to your industry.

- **Object-oriented programming**—A method of preparing parts of computer applications in which programmers develop a series of small programs, each of which performs a discrete task. These modules can be used repeatedly by a variety of programs. To create a software application or program, programmers link these generic modules together. This same approach underlies the mass-customization of information.

- **Portal**—Special Web pages that organize access to all of the online resources about a topic, providing a one-stop shop of sorts; a gateway to information sources and analysis tools for decision makers at appropriate places in an organization. Portals give real-time, single-point-of-access to the wealth of information and tools located both inside and outside the organization. Portals may present information from a broad array of sources such as project databases, data warehouses, and reports, presentations, emails, and external content providers. Portals may also support collaboration by giving users access to collaboration tools that link corporate experts and industry communities.

- **Profiling software**—Programs that assist organizations in describing users with minimal direct involvement of those users. These descriptions are called profiles.

- **Server computers**—Central computers that most users within the organization have access to. Firms typically store commonly used data and programs on servers, such as price lists, employee directories, and training courses.

- **Single sourcing**—The act of displaying online or printing information from the same file (called the source).

- **Single-sourcing tools**—Software that lets developers prepare a single source file of data and display it in a number of ways online and in print. Adobe's Portable Document Format (PDF) is one such tool.

- **Steering committee or council of senior executives**—A cross-functional team that represents respected thought leaders throughout the organization, typically made up of the highest-level officers of the organization. The purpose of the steering committee is to: provide funding, run interference, sign off on knowledge management initiatives, and promote knowledge sharing throughout the enterprise.

- **Structural capital**—The power-wielding knowledge that remains when employees leave.
- **Tacit knowledge**—Knowledge that resides in the minds of individuals and is surfaced in response to a situation or action.
- **Taxonomy**—On Web sites and portals, a site's taxonomy is its classification, or how it organizes its data into categories and subcategories. Taxonomies can be displayed in a site map, a model of a Web site's pages. Similar to tables of contents, site maps help users find information without having to navigate through all of the site's pages. (source: webopedia.com.)
- **Usability**—The ease and speed with which people can find information and the accuracy of their interpretation and application of that information.
- **XML, extended markup language**—A successor technology to the markup language HTML that lets developers prepare information as small chunks that can be mixed and matched at the time it is displayed online.

R E S O U R C E S

APQC provides many resources for knowledge management practitioners and executives.

1. **Annual knowledge management conferences**—Conducted at least once a year, APQC's knowledge management conferences present fresh cases and tools for knowledge management practitioners.

2. **Best-practice consortium benchmarking studies**—APQC has developed an award-winning methodology for its consortium benchmarking studies. Participants have saved millions of dollars by implementing best practices. APQC's research to date includes 11 major consortium benchmarking studies on knowledge management. The results are available in the following Best-practice Reports:
   - *Knowledge Management* (1996)
   - *Using Information Technology to Support Knowledge Management* (1997)
   - *Expanding Knowledge Management Externally: Putting Knowledge to Work for Customers* (1998)
   - *Knowledge Management and the Learning Organisation: A European Perspective* (1998)
   - *Creating a Knowledge-Sharing Culture* (1999)
   - *Successfully Implementing Knowledge Management* (2000)
   - *Building and Sustaining Communities of Practice* (2001)
   - *Managing Content and Knowledge* (2001)
   - *Retaining Valuable Knowledge: Proactive Strategies to Deal with a Shifting Work Force* (2002)
   - *Using Knowledge Management to Drive Innovation* (2002)
   - *Measuring the Impact of Knowledge Management* (2003)
   - *Facilitated Transfer of Best Practices* (2004)
   - *Virtual Collaboration: Enabling Teams and Communities of Practice* (2004)

3. **Training**—APQC offers knowledge management and other training and learning opportunities designed to increase your awareness of knowledge management issues and options. Knowledge management certification is available on completion

of APQC's Connected Learning series, which is a CD-ROM collection geared to individual, on-demand use. Knowledge management training courses include:

- Knowledge Management 101: A Knowledge Management Overview,
- Building and Sustaining Communities of Practice,
- Knowledge Management: Strategies and Tactics for Business Results,
- Establishing Performance Measures,
- Knowledge Mapping, and
- Content and Knowledge Management Systems.

4. **Individually sponsored research and training**—Applying 25 years of researching, identifying, and implementing best practices, APQC works with individual organizations to transfer recognized methods for obtaining results and how to be successful. By becoming an APQC project sponsor, organizations get hands-on support for knowledge management, benchmarking, and quality improvement initiatives. In turn, members help APQC and other members by providing a forum for the practical implementation, refinement, and dissemination of APQC research findings.

5. **Publications**—APQC offers a wide range of publications that can help organizations break out of conventional thinking and excel with best practices. Example publications follow.

- APQC's Passport to Success series: *Communities of Practice* (2001)
- APQC's Passport to Success series: *Content Management* (2003)
- APQC's Passport to Success series: *Knowledge Management* (2000) by O'Dell
- APQC's Passport to Success series: *Stages of Implementation* (2000) by O'Dell
- *Capturing Critical Knowledge from a Shifting Work Force* (2003)
- *Expertise Locator Systems: Finding the Answers* (2004)
- *If Only We Knew What We Know: The Transfer of Internal Knowledge and Best Practice* (Free Press, 1998) by O'Dell

- *Knowledge Management: Lessons from the Leading Edge* (1998)
- *Next-generation Knowledge Management* (2001)
- *Showcasing Successful Knowledge Management Implementation* (2000)
- *Taking Knowledge and Best Practices to the Bottom Line* (2001)
- *The World Bank Profile: Best Practices in Knowledge Management* (2003)